GETTING A JOB

IN ARCHITECTURE

AND DESIGN

GETTING A JOB

IN ARCHITECTURE

AND DESIGN

DAVID W. PATTERSON

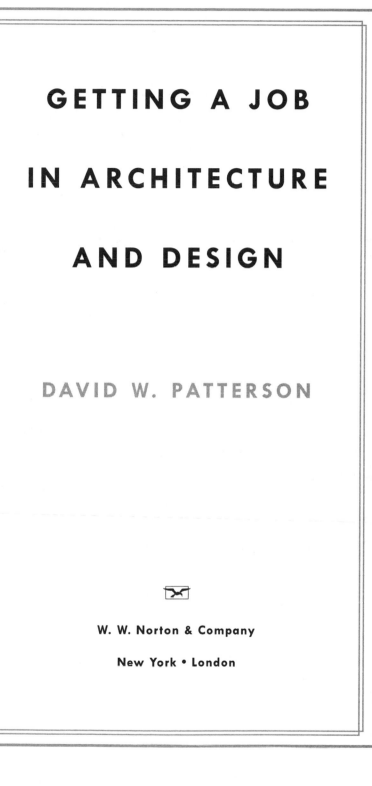

W. W. Norton & Company

New York • London

For information about permission to reproduce selections from this book,
write to Permissions, W. W. Norton & Company, Inc., 500 Fifth Avenue, New
York, NY 10110

For information about special discounts for bulk purchases, please contact
W. W. Norton Special Sales at specialsales@wwnorton.com or 800-233-4830

Manufacturing by Malloy Printing
Book design by Jonathan D. Lippincott
Production Manager: Leeann Graham

Library of Congress Cataloging-in-Publication Data
Patterson, David W.
    Getting a job in architecture and design / David W. Patterson. — 1st ed.
        p. cm.
    Includes index.
    ISBN 978-0-393-73217-7 (pbk.)
    1. Architecture—Vocational guidance. 2. Design—Vocational guidance.
I. Title.

NA1995.P29 2008
720.23—dc22   2007025229

ISBN 13: 978-0-393-73217-7 (pbk.)

W. W. Norton & Company, Inc., 500 Fifth Avenue, New York, N.Y. 10110
www.wwnorton.com

W. W. Norton & Company Ltd., Castle House, 75/76 Wells Street, London
W1T 3QT

0 9 8 7 6 5 4 3 2 1

CONTENTS

To Fran,

the patient one

GETTING A JOB

IN ARCHITECTURE

AND DESIGN

INTRODUCTION

The purpose of this book is to help architects, interior designers, and professionals in related fields—especially newcomers
to the profession—find rewarding employment. While having
contacts in the business can be of substantial value when looking for a job, in this book I make the assumption that you, the
job seeker, are not starting out with inside sources, and must
rely instead on your own determination to land a new position.
All job seekers within a particular area of specialization, with
comparable levels of experience and education, begin on an
even playing field.

Over the course of my career, I have searched for information to improve and expedite my job-hunting efforts, and have
found slim pickings in books about the design trades in general, and still less on individual disciplines such as architecture.
Most books concentrate on business, law, accounting, or other
"pinstripe suit" jobs (I, for one, can't stand pinstripes). This
book, therefore, is meant to offer what those other volumes do,
but also to go beyond them with information specific to architects and designers. My goal is to make it simpler, faster, less
painful, and possibly even enjoyable for those ambitious or un-
fortunate souls who, like myself, have to make an honest living,
and want to find the best way to do it!

Design, particularly architecture, has been referred to as

the "rich man's profession," due principally to the practitioners' heritage. This inaccurate label contributes to the difficult position in which many newcomers find themselves. Starting out designing luxurious weekend houses for affluent relatives is not the norm. The fact is, it does not take a rich person, nor a person who intends to become rich, to be successful in the field. Most design office employees remain middle class for the duration of their careers. It is possible to earn a comfortable living without ties to the principals, or winning the lottery. (Some of my former coworkers actually did win the lottery once, and they all remained at their jobs!) If you have persistence, drive, intelligence, and talent, given enough time you are capable of landing a satisfying position. A little luck also helps.

This book is arranged in order of the tasks you must carry out in preparing and applying for a design-related job, and it assumes no previous professional job-hunting experience. I have tried to minimize technical jargon, while remaining specific enough to avoid ambiguity. I recommend this practice for novice designers in their job hunt as well.

The first step toward a new job is awareness of your goals. What type of work is meaningful and fulfilling—professionally, financially, and otherwise—for you? While it is less and less common for designers to stay with one employer for their entire career, or even a major part of it, it is still a good idea to assume longevity when applying for a job. Remain flexible throughout the job-hunting process; leave the widest range of job prospects open. Your tastes, habits, and circumstances can change over a relatively short period of time, affecting your professional goals. So, take the long view; know yourself and your likely natural progression over time, not just at a given moment. Architecture, like most professions, continues to change in response to socio-economic, political, and cultural needs and trends. Design professions are in an especially rapid state of transition. Three major reasons for the fast pace of change are:

the need to speed up and better control the design process;

the rapid expansion of CAD and other technology; and

the growing popularity of the design-build movement.

Design clients want more from us sooner, better, and more cheaply than before.

Design professionals have not been serious political lobbyists historically, so they were, and still are, more at the mercy of economic trends than other groups, and they don't like it. They want more control. It is this desire to control, or at least influence, the construction industry that has brought about changes in professional practice. The winners will be those who can best re-mold their conventional wisdom into a new, third-millennium vision, in which designers also act as builders.

The point is that job-seekers should be mindful of the current state of the profession. You will be all the more enlightened, and may earn added bonuses, by being able to predict new directions and regroup to follow them. Deciding on directions, setting and prioritizing tasks, and establishing career goals are among the most difficult undertakings you will face. Make your own decisions by organizing all your ideas into one comprehensive plan, just as you would a design project. Don't be swayed by strong personalities, career counselors, or placement officers. They won't be doing your job. You will.

EXPECT UPS AND DOWNS

Even the best job-hunting efforts can be tough during downturns in the economy. You may have little choice but to temporarily put aside your wish list and accept the first reasonable opportunity that comes along. Staying flexible and creative will help you manage these situations.

This book is not only a manual, but an encouragement toward finding satisfaction as you enter a difficult profession. Statistics are appropriate to some careers, but they are of questionable value in professions noted for their artistic bent. Most of the material covered in this book comes from my own experience or that of colleagues, both during and between jobs. Most designers prefer to work (and play) hard, and do not enjoy periods of unemployment, yet unemployment, short or long, is a fact of many of our lives. While I am hopeful that changes in the field will benefit all of us with greater job stability, expect turnover to be an occasional part of your design career. It is good practice to prepare for the rainy day *and* the sunny day. There is always a silver lining, if not a welcome deliverance, in a new job. Good luck!

RULE #1: DON'T GIVE UP!

ONE

GETTING STARTED

"Some designers are born great, some achieve greatness, and some have greatness thrust upon them."
—William Shakespeare (paraphrased from *Twelfth Night*)

If you are not blessed with royal birth or ennobling quirks of fate, then the surest path to greatness is to achieve it—beginning with getting a job. Starting a job search may seem daunting, especially if it is your first time around or if you have not had the pleasure in a while. There are people to contact, resumes and letters to write, job ads to peruse, and meetings and interviews to set up. These are all necessary tasks to be undertaken in due time.

The first task in starting a job search is: Put yourself in the right mindset. The more focused you are on landing a new position, the quicker you will find one that matches your desires. While tunnel vision is usually not required, your best attention must be properly fixed on the *active* job search. Anxiety may affect your thought processes (which is okay), but try not to let negative emotions sway you from the main event.

RULE #2: DON'T PANIC!

The three most common reasons to conduct a job search are:

You are entering the job market, or a particular field within it (in this case design) for the first time.

You want to find a more advanced, and generally more lucrative, position in the same or related field.

You are unemployed due to involuntary termination by your employer from a previous position.

Other reasons for searching include a return to the job market after an extended hiatus such as child-rearing, a change in marital status, an extended medical leave, changes in financial needs, or the dissolution of the firm at which you worked.

While the differences between job-hunting techniques among these various situations are relatively minor, the differences in the attitudes taken by a potential employer can be considerable. For example, any employer approaches a job interview with an entry-level applicant differently from an interview with an experienced applicant. So it is valuable for you to adopt an employer's mindset, based on your professional and personal history.

RULE #3: KNOW YOURSELF.

Once you are mentally geared up, it is time to start making some fundamental decisions. Make the easy ones first and work your way up to the more difficult ones. Allow yourself time to prioritize your tasks. Answer these questions early on:

Why am I looking for a job?

When do I want to start a new job and, if currently employed, when do I want to quit?

Do I want to work full or part-time?

Do I want a permanent or temporary position?

Do I want to work in the private or public sector?

Do I want to work for a small, medium, or large firm?

Do I want to work for a firm whose main purpose is design or construction?

Do I want, or am I willing, to relocate?

While these questions may seem simple, the answers are very important to prospective employers, and may limit or expand your job options.

THE RIGHT JOB, NOT JUST ANY JOB

Getting the *right* design job is key, and you will get it if you understand the employer's needs, they understand yours, and you are both willing to do what it takes to establish common ground and a good working relationship. When job hunting, accept that the process will not be a linear one, and that no one will make it easy for you.

The cast of characters involved is worthy of a novel. Design employers are naturally quirky. They can be volatile, arrogant, abusive, and irresponsible. They can also be sensitive, earthy, and hard-working. More than a few are paranoid, and most are chronically afraid of running out of work. And then there are the general types to be found in the field.

There are those foiled or would-be fine artists, who often concentrate on the front end of a project. Their primary concern is not schedules or budgets. Some know that computers can help their practice, but they haven't a clue how they work. These cutting-edge designers tend to think theoretically and outside the box. They control the overall direction of the office. They aspire to high-end projects, such as museums and theaters.

Others in the field are design-conscious, with an eye to

consistency throughout the design process. They do not, how-ever, belabor the slightest details or attempt to re-invent the wheel with each new project. They know a head joint from a bed joint, and follow accepted business principles. They share office control and direction with staff. Their work consists of quality commercial, residential, and institutional design.

Still other designers are production-oriented, and just want to crank out as much work as possible as quickly as possible. Quality of design matters little to them, and their clients feel the same way. There is little by way of detailing in their work; free thought is o.k., as long as it doesn't get in the way. These designers generally work on warehouses, industrial plants, housing sub-developments, and in support service to engi-neers and builders.

Corporate and public employers see design purely as a sup-port service, creative though it may also happen to be. Their primary interests are not in buildings for themselves, but as a practical means to an end. They are concerned with deliver-able products: goods, services, and administration. Designers fill important slots, but aren't ordinarily concerned with policy or executive decisions. Non-designers run this show.

All of these types of employers are legitimate, and can pro-vide agreeable work environments. Is there risk? Of course. But holding out for an exact match is the biggest risk of all; there is no walk-in perfect design job. The key is to find a po-tentially promising employer, and then grow into the job, based on your and your employer's needs and interests. This takes time and patience, and it may not always be fun. But, the successful employees in most offices are the ones who stuck out the initial hardships and carved an essential professional niche for themselves. Their office needs them. They remain committed and enthusiastic about the design process, and see projects through, soup to nuts.

They get it. So should you. As a result, when applying for a position, always remember: the WORK comes first, the OF-

FICE comes second, YOU come last. The most common cause of dissatisfaction among employees *and* employers is neglect of this principle. Plum projects do not equal a plum job, and vice versa. Knowing this from the outset will help you remain open yet focused. Show employers that *you* understand it.

YOUR FIRST PROFESSIONAL JOB

If you are old enough to remember the adage, "Want a job? Get experience. Want experience? Get a job" then you are probably not looking for your first design job. But this Catch-22 still holds for newcomers to the field. Most commonly, job hunters have recently completed their professional education. This is a time of excitement as well as anxiety. If you had part-time or temporary experience with a design or other firm while in school, you will have a better understanding of professional office practices than colleagues who have not. Still, the challenge of finding work is compounded by having to decide what type of lifestyle you wish to maintain, now and in the foreseeable future. Be realistic throughout this process, and take stock of your desires, strengths and weaknesses. It is not a requirement that every entry-level job applicant be humble, nor that all newcomers ask for low wages. As with job seekers at all levels, you have to ascertain and take your proper place in the lineup.

There are generally more jobs available for those at entry and lower levels than there are for those, say, with ten or more years of experience, but competition can be intense nonetheless. Schools are producing designers in greater numbers, and attempting to separate yourself from the starting pack can be difficult without professional experience. Employers' desks are habitually stacked high with resumes from novice applicants. More on this will be covered in chapter four, but keep in mind that school is vastly different from the workplace, and that the mental adjustment from one situation to the other may be more difficult for recent graduates than for those already in the field.

If you are entering the design field for the first time, but have had previous experience in another area in an earlier career, the same basic principles apply. The mental adjustment, however, may not be as severe. You will have an edge over new job-market entrants, in part based on greater maturity, but you will have to be just as realistic. Someone with ten years' experience in another business will not achieve the same seniority level as would someone with ten years in design. It may, however, help a bit; at least a prospective employer knows that the experienced applicant can do *something*. Second-career applicants should review their professional credentials, and extract and feature any that may support them in the design workplace. Tasks including supervision, scheduling, and budgeting are all good starters.

CHANGING JOBS

Of all the reasons for wanting a new job, changing jobs is perhaps the "cushiest." No matter how onerous, tedious, low paying, or inconvenient one's job is, it is generally better to keep it while looking for another. Quitting a job without first landing another is seldom a good idea. People used to change jobs for more fulfilling work, greater seniority or higher wages; this practice has, at least in part, changed recently. Now, many people change jobs because they *anticipate* these needs. Their employer merged with another firm, resulting in too much overlap; their employer was bought by another firm, and "house cleaning" has started; the shareholders are complaining of low profits, and management must downsize; or, employees foresee the imminent end of the market in their sector. While some of these occurrences may be less common among design firms, they nonetheless affect designers. They certainly affect clients. Most areas of design still respond to fluctuations in other industries, and design firms must anticipate these changes.

If you are seeking a new job for the conventional reasons of more fulfilling work, more seniority or more money, great! Those currently employed are in the best negotiating position, and can hold out for the best assignments and wages. The job market is always in need of ambitious, enthusiastic people to keep it dynamic, progressive, and vibrant.

Job seekers who wish to leave one job for another should be careful to ascertain the current and future workload of a potential new employer, especially if they have been at their present job for some time. No one having left a job after ten years will want to see a new one run dry after six months. Unless a temporary position is desired, verify a workload-outlook of at least one year with a prospective new employer. If possible, estimate the projected workload of your current employer and compare.

JOB-HUNTING WHILE UNEMPLOYED

Looking for a job while not working is never something to be ashamed of. The most common cause of unemployment is involuntary termination. Employers know this, and have probably experienced it at some earlier point in their careers. Indeed, I suspect that many set up shop on their own following such severance. During economic downturns, the majority of those in the job market may be unemployed, and those with jobs will be hesitant about leaving them. Employers know this too, but it does not seem to affect their speed in the selection and hiring process. Be prepared for a wait, especially if you are seeking a senior position.

Job seekers on financially shaky ground must be especially

efficient and act with dispatch. Not only do they have to prove themselves to potential employers; they have to do it *quickly*. It is fine to take the "deluge the market" approach during this time, and send resumes to every design firm in the western hemisphere. Occasionally this works for lower-level positions, but it is of limited value at middle and upper levels. In any case, if you are terminated, immediately review your financial status and determine how long you can realistically afford to be out of work. Consider your expenses and spending habits, and plan for a period of belt-tightening as needed. Someone who needs a new job within six weeks has more incentive to be listed with employment agencies than someone who can hold out for six months. You have to adjust the priorities and tasks of your job hunt according to your circumstance. Staying flexible throughout is key.

ALL APPLICANTS

Regardless of your particular status as a job seeker, think about your place in the professional hierarchy—your desires, goals and experience—early on. There are levels of design positions within each firm, and an unofficial hierarchy among firms. The prominence of a firm affects its attitude toward job applicants. Large firms and those noted for consistently high-quality design have reputations that precede them; unsolicited resumes flow in on a continuous basis, and competition for jobs is the toughest (internal competition is usually also toughest). Smaller and less well-known firms receive fewer unsolicited resumes, but probably have fewer job openings. The nature of a firm's work, especially if it concentrates on a particular area of design within its field, also affects hiring practices. Firms specializing in a particular design segment often seek out applicants who have both a solid general background *and* a specialized background.

RULE #4: KNOW YOUR COMPETITION.

Coming to grips with your professional capabilities, along with your aspirations, helps establish where you belong in the hierarchy within the field, a particular area of design, and an individual firm. Some aspects of competition within the field can be taken in through osmosis, but you will pick up many more as part of your research.

TWO

JOB RESEARCH

"Research is the process of going up alleys to see if they are blind."
—Marston Bates

Looking for a job in any field requires research. Looking for a job in a field of design arguably requires even more research than many other professions. By now, you should have assessed your position in relation to the job market, and have an idea of professional—and realistic—goals and desires. Your efforts will become progressively more focused on a few, concentrated aspects of the market. The more data you gather about the state of the market, the greater the number of potential opportunities open to you. This chapter helps you sort through the overwhelming array of options and hone a targeted and efficient job-hunting strategy.

RULE #5: RECORD EVERYTHING.

Until you find—and start—your new job, always have a pad and pen (or laptop) by your side. No one has ever kept excessive records as part of a job-hunting effort. Maintain a telephone/fax/e-mail log. Be orderly: Set up formats for recording each task (e.g., telephone calls, online searches, interviews), whether on paper or on disk. All such records should include:

the date;

the name, telephone number, and e-mail address
   of the contact;

topics of discussion;

follow-up required (if any); and

the names of any referrals.

The more structured your job-hunting activities are, the quicker they will yield results. So, once your record-keeping system is up and running (you can modify it over time), it is time to get physical. While research techniques vary based on the type of job desired, and individual preference, those strategies applicable to the widest range of the design job market are:

online research;

reviewing trade publications;

use your colleagues;

networking and conferences;

non-Internet job listings;

understanding contract employment

minority opportunities; and

spotting current trends.

Answering help-wanted ads and contacting employment agencies will be covered later. We are still on the research track, and the goal is to find out what is going on in the field, and where. This is critical to establishing your priorities and direction. If banks are where the money is, then busy areas of design are where the work is. Let's take a closer look at these methods.

ONLINE RESEARCH

Internet-based job hunting is now the rule, and what used to take hours and days of typing, retyping, printing, copying, and mailing can now be handled with a few keystrokes.

We are entering an epoch when no design firm will be without a Web site. This phenomenon is a boon to job-seeking designers. As in all other job-hunting tasks, however, the goal of the Internet search is the same: how to obtain and use the best job-related information with the least effort. So, what do you need to do to achieve this?

Answer: Find the best Web sites. For information on searches using the Internet, there is *The Guide to Internet Job Searching* (Riley, Roehm & Oserman, 1997; VGM Career Horizons).

To conduct a Web search, start with a name or subject, and look it up. Most browsers offer access to search engines, a good place to start any type of job search. The URLs for some major search engines are:

www.google.com
www.yahoo.com
www.altavista.com
www.northernlight.com
www.go.com
www.excite.com
www.hotbot.com
www.lycos.com
www.ask.com
www.about.com

In general, the first four are the best for design firm and organization links; expect to use them regularly.

Commercial Job Web Sites

There are also commercial, organizational, and publicly-sponsored Web sites that specialize in job vacancies. Commercial sites offer jobs in numerous, varied professions in locations countrywide—indeed, worldwide. Most categorize jobs by profession and duties, but some also sort by location. Major commercial sites include the following:

www.hotjobs.com
www.careerpath.com
www.monster.com
www.craigslist.com
www.classifiedventures.com
www.careerbuilder.com
www.vault.com
www.sixfigurejobs.com
www.jobsonline.com
www.careersonline.com

Each asks you to enter a description of the position sought. Be as specific as possible without ruling out possible matches. Other industries have adopted design terminology; so entering "architect" or "designer" may take you to listings for positions unrelated to buildings. Proper descriptive adjectives and "helper" words can streamline this process substantially. For example, try:

architect building design "new york"
architect OR "interior designer" buildings chicago
architect OR "interior designer" NOT computer
architect OR "interior designer" CAD "santa fe"
architect "historic preservation" london uk
"facilities planning" OR "facilities management"
    FFE toronto canada

Such general job sites are usually run by major conglomerates of employment recruiters, and they tend to work by offering sheer volume, not personal attention. Still, they can be useful for assessing the types of positions available at major firms. Use email subscriptions that will contact you when positions matching your search criteria are posted.

Public Job Websites

Branches of federal, state, and local government maintain Web sites, including job databases for both public and private positions. The federal Department of Labor (DOL) sponsors a jobs database: www.usajobs.opm.gov. Click on "Related Sites/Indexes of State & Local Government Information/[Individual State]". To look for public announcements of jobs in your own or another state, try going through the state's Web site, www.[name of state].gov. Job listing is usually a subcategory, accessible from a click-heading (e.g., "Employment Opportunities; Recruitment"). If no such choice is presented, then go to the Department of Labor's Web site: www.dol.gov.

Public Announcements

Web sites listing public solicitations for design services, requests for proposals, and qualifications, are a good place to look for names and addresses of potential employers, and very often the name of a contact person at the firms. Try searching:

> *Commerce Business Daily/CBD*, cbdnet.access.gpo
>   .gov
> *Brown's Letters*, www.brownsletters.com
> *Bid Clerk*, www.bidclerk.com

Many public design contracts are awarded through these listings—and for prestigious projects. The firms submitting the best proposals are short-listed and interviewed for the commission, which will be awarded to one of them. Reviewing these sites cues you in to the competitive markets among design firms and their clients. If there are listings for potentially interesting projects, it may be worthwhile to follow up with the project sponsor to find out which firm got the job, and add that firm's name to your list of job prospects. This process takes time, and is not for those who need to find a job pronto.

Dedicated Job Web Sites

We are getting more specific. Professional interest groups, such as the American Institute of Architects (AIA) and the American Society of Interior Designers (ASID), sponsor dedicated job listings principally for the benefit of their members and others in the field. Their job-related information is almost exclusively attuned to the interests of designers, and should be among the first resources used in a job search. The following sites have career-related info and/or job listings:

> AIA: www.aia.org
> ASID: asid.jobcontrolcenter.com

Other more general sites include:

> www.e-architect.com
> www.archizilla.com
> www.managementdesign.com
> www.reedcontructiondata.com
> www.architecturalrecord.com
> www.jobs.architectjobsonline.com
> www.interiordesign.net
> www.interiordesignjobs.com
> www.iida.org
> www.architectsusa.com
> www.internationaljobs.org

Note that membership in AIA, ASID and other professional organizations may be required for access to certain "privileged" Web site subcategories. In some instances, you may be referred to a local or state chapter Web site or office for more detailed career information. Other organizational Web sites may concentrate on one or a few locations, such as a particular state. Try them all—you may find useful links.

Internships

If you are seeking an internship, not a full-time paid position, organizational Web sites are also helpful. The nationwide program for architecture is the Intern Development Program (IDP), administered by the National Council of Architectural Registration Boards (NCARB; www.ncarb.org/idp). For interior design, it is the Interior Design Experience Program (IDEP), administered by the National Council for Interior Design Qualifications (NCIDQ; www.ncidq.org/idep.htm). The AIA's internship program can be viewed at: www.aia.org/idp. For general information on internships, see: www.internjobs .com, www.internshipprograms.com or www.internweb.com.

Employer Web Sites

Obtaining and making good use of the Web sites of individual potential employers is the most specific—and valuable—goal in your Internet job search. Some firms even accept applications directly through their site, with a fill-in-the-blanks form, or through an e-mail link. At least they will tell you where to mail or fax a resume; or you can click on "Contact Us" and send an inquiring e-mail.

The following are some rules of etiquette for communicating directly with a potential employer through its Web site:

> Unless you are instructed otherwise, forward resumes directly to the office(s) you would like to work in, national or international. Most Web

sites furnish addresses of all of a firm's locations. If not, send it to the firm's headquarters office (see appendices for a list of large firms).

Large firms may list job openings in several categories, such as career applicants, school year interns, and summer job apprentices. Do not apply for a job in more than one category at a time.

All sites feature some information about the firm, such as its history, design philosophy, clientele, partner biographies, and examples of projects. Review these before forwarding a resume. If you reference projects of particular interest, or can customize your resume to suit the firm, your Web-surfing time will have been worthwhile. Whether you send it by e-mail or regular mail, your resume is still your introduction to a potential employer. Do not abbreviate it or make it less formal for e-mail purposes. Remember, your resume must stand out among the resumes flowing into most offices. (See chapter four for more on resumes.)

Some employers will not accept resumes as attachments to e-mail messages. E-mail attachments other than a resume, such as photos and drawings, should not be sent with an initial submission—whether e-mail or hard copy—unless specifically requested. In both cases, differences in software may make opening attachments, written or graphic, difficult or impossible; do not rely on them. Do follow instructions.

If you have your own Web site, include a link to it in your mail to the firm. Do not, however, count on someone on the other end to visit it, and do not put critical resume material solely on your

Web site. Key material should still be included in your primary correspondence.

So, whom should you contact? Start with the firms listed in appendices A, B, C, and D, especially if you prefer large employers. Or draw from your own list. Look at trade journals and newsletters to see who is doing what in and beyond your region.

How to Search

Like anything, practice makes perfect, and the ins and outs of Web site searching are easy to learn. The Internet is filled with eccentricities, but there are ways around them. Be tenacious, and you will enjoy a high success rate (mine is 95 percent, and I'm no Web geek). Finding a Web site can involve one step or ten (foreign firms especially). Keep a detailed record of all relevant Web site addresses—you'll need them later. Here's how to start:

1. Try www.google.com. Enter only the name of the firm, and click on "Google Search." If the name of the firm in question is Vitruvius, Callicrates & Associates, Architects PC, just enter "vitruvius callicrates associates." (Do not include quotation marks unless you intend to search only for the exact phrase contained within them.) Capitalization is not required, and punctuation (commas, ampersands, etc.) is discouraged. With luck, the firm will appear immediately at the top of the list of search results. Click on the blue heading to go directly to the site. The search can end here. If not, go back and start over.

2. Re-enter the name of the firm, adding more information, such as the location: "vitruvius calli-

crates associates new york." This may narrow down the search results to more relevant sites. It is surprising how many firms there are with similar names, especially ones that go by initials (SOM, HOK, HNTB). If this does not yield satisfactory results, try step 3.

3. Even if your target firm is not listed with its own Web site, it may be referred to in another listing, such as a trade journal Web site, or Web sites featuring listings of design firms in a particular region, such as www.resources.com/architects. These secondary sources, such as articles about the firm, or its geographical location, can yield important information. If you find an e-mail address, use it to inquire if the firm has a Web site, or reconfigure the address itself as a Web site link. For example, if the e-mail address for Vitruvius & Callicrates Associates is office@vcaa.com, try: www.vcaa.com.

4. Do not assume an international firm has no Web site just because searches on a search engine yielded no results. Most large foreign firms maintain their own Web sites and are as accessible as American firms if you know how and where to look. Different areas of the world have their own Web address standards, and it may be necessary to enter the country code in the Web site address, for example:
   • www.[name of firm].co.uk (for United Kingdom)
   • www.[name of firm].de (for Germany)
   • www.[name of firm].se (for Sweden)
   • www.[name of firm].jp (for Japan)

In the case of Asian firms, or any that do not use the Latin alphabet, extra care is needed. Web site text in Asian, Arabic, or Cyrillic may come

up as unintelligible, garbled symbols and require supplemental software for viewing. Some
have an alternate English-language version of
the website. If not, try entering a suffix, for example, www.[nameoffirm].jp/english. Occasionally it scores.

5. If you know where a firm is located, you can always look up their phone number in a traditional
phone book and call for more information. Start
with the toll-free directory (1-800-555-1212);
you may save a long distance call. If you plan to
do a lot of cold calling, consider a prepaid
phone card, the costs of which are tax-deductible.

If the firm simply does not have a Web site, do not write it off. Even a few of the top 100 firms lack Web sites. So, print out a hard copy, put a stamp on an envelope, and . . . well, you know the rest.

REVIEWING TRADE PUBLICATIONS

Trade journals, reviews, newsletters and books help keep you familiar with the current state of international, national, and local developments in your field. Do not rely on electronic editions of journals or other media: get the comprehensive print version if possible. Be aware that the trendier a publication is, the sooner an issue is likely to become outdated. So, read recent issues.

Trade Journals

Some trade journals include job listings, but the main reason to review a journal is to learn about the most active, best funded, or otherwise most important activities in the field, especially in the context of larger socio-economic and political trends. Sometimes articles yield concrete indications of directions, sometimes the topics covered may seem of passing interest. For a full understanding of the state of design, however, you need both broad and specific design coverage. The more journals you read, the more you will know. Watch for discussions of:

> legal aspects of design trades (especially professional liability);
> comparisons between personnel practices and policies from firm to firm;
> new developments in design-related computer technology,
> environmentally conscious design and its proponents; and
> disaster relief and control.

Do not focus on one phenomenon or flashy trend. Save the articles or record topics that interest you; if a project description warrants further investigation, make a note of its nature and location, the design firm(s) and its location, and what distinguishes it (e.g., form, materials, client). These notes give you leads to firms you can contact. Look for announcements of recently awarded contracts that include the name of the designer, another source of job potential.

Major journals to review include:

> *Architectural Record* (AIA affiliate) Published by McGraw-Hill
> 2 Penn Plaza
> New York, NY 10121-2298
> www.architecturalrecord.com

(877) 876-8093
$49.00/year; 12 issues

Architect Magazine
Published by Hanley-Wood, LLC
One Thomas Circle, NW
Washington, DC 20005
www.architectmagazine.com
(202) 452-0800
Free to the trade; 12 issues

World Architecture
Published by The Builder Group
Anchorage House, 7th Floor
2 Clove Crescent
London E14 2BE, UK
www.world-architecture.com
+44 (0) 20 7560 4000
Free to *bd* magazine subscribers; $24.90/issue
    for mail order (from the U.K.)

ENR
Published by McGraw-Hill
2 Penn Plaza
New York, NY 10121-2298
www.enr.com
(877) 876-8208
$82.00/year; 50 issues

ICON (ASID publication)
Published by Hanley-Wood, LLC
608 Massachusetts Avenue, NE
Washington, DC 20002-6006
www.asid.org/knowledge/ICON.htm

(612) 904-7249
Free with ASID membership; 6 issues

Interiors & Sources
Published by L.C. Clark
840 US Highway One, Suite 330
North Palm Beach, FL 33408
www.isdesignet.com
(800) 556-2632
Free; 11 issues

Interior Design
Published by Reed Business Info
P.O. Box 5662
Harlan, IA 51593-1162
www.interiordesign.net
(800) 900-0804
$69.99/year; 15 issues

designbuild (DBIA publication)
Published by McGraw-Hill
144 Lexington St.
Woburn, MA 01801
www.designbuildmag.com
(877) 876-8208
Distributed quarterly to subscribers of *Architectural Record* and *ENR*.

Newsletters

State and local chapters of national trade organizations such as AIA and ASID publish newsletters on a regular basis. Local newsletters are a must if you want to keep your job-hunting local. They report on the projects of local firms, and often interweave this information with local political news or other events that may influence local design practices. They frequently also include a calendar of professional events. If you do not already subscribe to a newsletter, you may still be able to purchase individual copies, or subscribe as a non-member. The cost is usually minimal.

Newspapers

Newspapers, especially in metropolitan areas, sometimes run feature articles on recent developments in design—particularly projects with high-profile clients, such as cultural organizations, schools, government agencies, and celebrity clients. Newspapers have a different take than trade journals and newsletters, perhaps emphasizing a project's social relevance, or its unusual style. Such coverage is worth reading for its perspective, and the other topics it may introduce as background and rationale for current design trends.

Books

Books provide valuable background for particular types of design and designers, and are most useful for researching past works of a particular designer or firm over an extended time period. If you plan to apply to a well-known office, and know little about its history, look it up in a reference volume or portfolio collection. Both technical and popular books are also helpful for research and can be found in your local library or bookstore, or through Internet vendors.

USE YOUR COLLEAGUES

You very well might have associates, friends, relatives, or former classmates in or near your chosen field, maybe more than you realize. Getting in touch with them is a good way to start your search. Conveniently, you can do this outside of regular business hours.

Tell your contacts that you are in the job market. Try to keep discussions low-key; do not start off by recounting your dire financial straits, even if you are desperate. Do not dismiss anything told to you as silly or irrelevant. Some of the best and most imaginative design assignments can come from what seem, at first, crazy ideas. Remember our field is naturally quirky!

Before contacting colleagues, make a list of the topics to discuss and record their responses to each item—without advertising that you are doing so! Some openings to try are:

> How is your job going, and what is your office up to?
>
> Is your office busy? If so, is your firm looking to hire additional staff?
>
> May I send you a resume to be forwarded to your office's personnel department?
>
> Do you know of any other firms which are busy and/or looking to hire?
>
> Do you know if your firm uses placement services? If so, which?
>
> Have you recently heard from anyone in [common trade organization, common school, common former office, etc.]? What are they up to?
>
> Are you attending the upcoming trade gathering on [subject]?
>
> Did you read the recent article in [trade publication] on future trends in the profession (or whatever)? What is your take on it?

Even professionals in design areas other than your own can provide valuable information, and expose you to aspects of a related field you may not have considered. When in doubt, call.

NETWORKING AND CONFERENCES

Attending conferences, conventions, lectures, demonstrations, and other trade gatherings may be a luxury if you are not working or if your employer does not offer paid leave or reimbursement. However, attending such events is worthwhile, not only for what you may learn about the announced topic or purpose of the meeting, but as an opportunity to make professional contacts—networking. Not all of these events are pricey (and fees may be tax-deductible), and some are free. They are frequently held during off-hours. Go!

Talking to colleagues at gatherings will introduce you to others, who, in turn, can lead you to still more new contacts. Networking can be the backbone of your research, as it is for firms in getting clients, and can be approached in much the same way. Indeed, many employees have become self-employed by using networking skills in their spare time and finding their own work. The practice may seem obvious, but most design professionals underuse it.

Trade gatherings usually schedule time for informal discussion among attendees. Arrive a little early and be ready to stay a little late, so you can use this time to make, and re-establish, contacts. Always start out with a low-key topic, such as the subject of the gathering, or other pleasantries, before mentioning that you are in the job market. Then cover the following:

> your area of preference and expertise;
> your acquaintance's place of employment and
>   area of expertise;
> your contact information (study the other person's
>   to remember him/her and convey that you are
>   genuinely interested. Review all cards received
>   after the event, and make further notations as
>   required);
> the names of others who may be able to help you;

upcoming events worth attending; and
the exchange of business cards.

If you do not have employer-provided cards, have your own printed (which is not expensive). If the card does not indicate what you do, write it on the back. Keep the business cards you collect in an orderly fashion. If not printed on the card, note the person's job title for future reference.

Follow-up calls to people you have met recently at trade gatherings are acceptable, but use discretion. Once in the networking groove, it is easier to talk to acquaintances new and old, to work job-hunting topics into your discussions automatically, and to know your competition.

I have found most colleagues and acquaintances willing to assist a job hunter; some will even make inquiries on your behalf. Virtually everyone has looked for a job, and knows the routine. Good networking leads to better jobs—often jobs that are not advertised. Remember the help you get, and hopefully soon you will be on the giving end.

NON-INTERNET JOB LISTINGS

Newspaper classified ads, professional placement services, contract employers, Civil Service and other public job listings tend to have a broader selection of positions than trade publications do. Some of these services are available online or in trade publications, but most are widely available in print.

Newspaper Ads

Major daily newspapers are still a good source of print listings of design and design-related jobs. Remember to look beyond the basic headings for "Architect" or "Interior Designer." Other possible headings include:

project manager;
construction manager;
facilities planner/manager;
space planner;
CAD operator/drafter; or
engineer.

Job listings are not limited to "Help Wanted" sections. For instance, the *New York Times* Sunday edition includes a separate "Money and Business" section, which often contains listings for technical and administrative design-related positions. These positions are frequently among the best available (or at least the best compensated).

Look at the fine print. Do not skip over a job ad just because it is headlined "Engineer" and you want a job as an architect. Architects can perform some tasks for which engineers may be solicited (e.g., project management, marketing, field supervision, estimating), and most employers will accept resumes from professionals in related fields if their backgrounds are consistent with the job description. Out-of-town job assignments may appear in local newspapers. Take a look—they are good indicators of what is going on elsewhere, and where there may be a labor shortage. If you are considering a job out-of-town, get a copy of a major newspaper from the closest urban area (some libraries and specialty news stands stock these). While checking and responding to help-wanted ads is always a valid and valuable means of looking, it is generally among the slowest in providing results. Do it anyway.

Private Ads

Specialist publishers issue periodically updated circulars with job listings. Examples include:

> Adams *Job Bank* series (Avon, MA; www.adamsmedia.com), in separate volumes covering different geographic areas of the country. *International Employment Hotline* (Oakton, VA; www.internationaljobs.org).

Browse through such publications at a library or a bookstore; different books will appeal to different job seekers. Make a note of or photocopy job listings of interest, and follow them up. Note the posting date and the job reference code, if any.

Phone Book

A traditional telephone directory can be a godsend or a nightmare. Cold calling the phone book's list of designers is one of the most common, simplest, and cheapest means of covering a lot of ground in a short time. You can get Web site and e-mail addresses, fax numbers, postal addresses and even names of contacts this way. Some firms will tell you they are not hiring; some will not give out the names of staff. Very few will put you through to the personnel director. More and more, those in charge of hiring do not want to take calls from job applicants. Accordingly, I advise *not* asking to speak to them until after you send your resume. Collect as much raw data from the receptionist/operator as possible, and add the information to your list of potential employers.

Placement Services

A common job search routine is to list yourself with professional placement services. Check phone book listings under "Employment Agencies" or "Personnel Consultants." Call to find out if the agency handles your specialty, and if so, the placement officer who covers that area. Names of additional agencies may be acquired from trade associations, and, of course, from colleagues. Find out who the heavy hitters are; stay in regular contact with them. More will be covered on this later.

Like agencies, contract employers list and find jobs. But instead of working directly for a design firm, you work for, and are paid by an intermediary company, which in turn, bills and is paid by the client firm to which you are assigned. Although historically oriented to short-term employment, medium and long-term assignments are becoming more commonly offered by contract employers because they offer flexibility, little or no term commitment, and relatively low overhead. In some branches of the design field (e.g., engineering and architecture), this arrangement is called a *job shop*; its employees job-shoppers. A bona-fide setup, it offers more flexibility than a normal position and can be ideal for filling gaps between permanent jobs, especially during hard times.

If you can't find many job shop listings on your own, you may be able to obtain additional ones from employment agents, through publications like *Contract Employment Weekly* (Kirkland, WA; www.ceweekly.com; note that you must subscribe to view online) or by talking to colleagues who have worked under this arrangement. If you are interviewing at a firm for a contract position, ask what other employment contractors it uses, and add them to your list.

Civil Service Listings

Looking for a civil service or other government job tests your bureaucratic management as well as your job research skills. Do not expect it to go smoothly or quickly. Putting together a public sector job list may turn out to be the easiest part of the hunt. Be prepared to fill in plenty of blanks on lengthy applications, to provide proof of education and/or license, and even to take a written placement exam.

One advantage, however, of government bureaucracy is that many federal agencies list you as an eligible candidate. Federal job listings are found at federal offices or in publications such as *Federal Career Opportunities* (Vienna, VA; www.fedjobs.com), which can be ordered from the Department of Labor in Washington, D.C. (200 Constitution Ave. NW, Washington, D.C. 20210).

State job listings are usually available at any state Department of Labor office, particularly those handling unemployment claims. They may also be found in *America's Job Bank* (U.S. Department of Labor, Oakton, VA; www.jobbankinfo.com).

Local government and other public-agency job listings are available at county and municipal offices, and Town Halls.

Submitting a general, multi-departmental (and multi-disciplinary) federal or state employment application is a start, but results tend to be slow in coming. Since job openings may not be nearby, this method is best when considering a job out-of-town. For any local public employer it is much more expeditious to deal directly with individual departments and agencies, virtually all of which maintain their own separate human resources staffs.

Public job offices have facilitated job searching by computerizing their job banks. If you do not see a computer terminal at a public counter that will yield a listing or printout of current job openings, ask an agent about it. Some listings in state and local government offices include private-sector jobs. They include annual or hourly wages for each position.

UNDERSTANDING CONTRACT EMPLOYMENT

This fast-growing type of professional employment may or may not be for you, but it is worthwhile to consider. Contract employment can accommodate many lifestyles, but tends to be best suited to those:

> who are single;
> who are mobile;
> for whom job security is not critical;
> who like job flexibility and/or job variety;
> who prefer certain days or weeks off; or
> want higher wages than permanent jobs offer.

Contract employment is usually for temporary positions, and paid by hour. Job shops have staffing agreements with any number of clients, and some specialize in design services. Examples of contract employer Web sites are:

> www.aejob.com
> www.ceweekly.com

www.sologig.com

jobsearchtech.about.com/od/contractjobs/

www.careers.org

www.spherion.com

Here's how contract employment works:

1. When a job order for a contract position comes in from a client, job shops search their files for resumes from applicants whose experience matches the client's requirements. Some shops specialize in local placement; some in out-of-town.

2. When they find a match, the rep contacts you the applicant to discuss the assignment, including the proposed hourly rate. If there is mutual interest, the rep forwards the resume to the client.

3. The client reviews the resume, and gives a yes or no answer. If yes, the job shop arranges for an interview.

4. A local interview would take place at the client's office; an out-of-town client may conduct interviews by phone.

5. The client considers you, and generally notifies the job shop of their decision; the job shop will in turn notify you.

6. The client makes an offer to the job shop, which in turn makes an offer to you.

7. If you accept, written agreements are sent to you to sign and return. You have officially become a job shopper, ready to start work. (Occasionally you can actually start work at an assigned office before all the paperwork is done.)

The job shop's contractual agreement includes terms and conditions of employment, the workweek, wages (including overtime rates), and duration of assignment, if predetermined. Most domestic assignments will not require a specific time commitment, just an *estimated*, but *not minimum*, length of service. Foreign assignment contracts frequently require a fixed or minimum term. In both cases, if the client requires a minimum term, the agreement with the job shop must assure one of equal or greater length. Be aware that contract agreements are for both the employer's *and* the employee's advantage. Most are brief and straightforward, and should be reviewed carefully. Don't hesitate to bring up items in the contract you are not clear on or comfortable with. There is generally no direct agreement between the client and the job-shopper.

In reality, as a contract employee, you can go for years on end without ever meeting your employers face-to-face. Timesheets are forwarded to the job shop, and the paychecks sent out. Contract employers generally place professional staff on the strength of their resume and basic phone discussions (Do you want to work in [place]?). Tailor your resume to contract work; emphasize your ability to pick up new assignments readily, and feature as many professional buzzwords as possible.

MINORITY OPPORTUNITIES

Many job ads include the phrase "Minorities encouraged to apply", or EOE (Equal Opportunity Employer). Since the 1970s, employers have been sensitive to the political and legal requirements of a balanced workforce. No U.S. employer can legally deny you a job because of your race or sex. Some employers, especially if they are public or do publicly funded work, are *required* to hire minorities. Nonetheless, *never* ask whether a position has been set aside for a minority or woman. This can be a sensitive issue to some employers. Approach each potential job as if every designer qualifies for it equally.

Minorities (and women) should research which employers are likely to reserve slots for them; some suggestions:

> **Design firms:** If the firm is large or doing public projects, it probably employs a steady minority workforce. (A minimum ratio of minorities and women is usually required for a publicly issued RFP.) Or, look for minority- or woman-owned firms. You can find lists of recognized DBE (Disadvantaged Business Enterprise) firms, including MBE (Minority Business Enterprise) and WBE (Women Business Enterprise) at state and local government offices and websites.
>
> **Corporations:** Most companies want to maintain a representative minority showing, both because their attorneys told them to, and because diversity has been shown to be good business practice. Their design departments' positions for minorities are among the most stable in the private sector. Again, firms with public customers or large customer bases make good starting points.
>
> **Government:** *All* government agencies—federal, state and local—hire minorities in greater numbers than private industry. Some jobs are reserved for minority applicants, and promotions after hiring are virtually guaranteed. Agencies with in-house design staffs will still evaluate minority applicants based on their experience and other qualifications, but the competition may be somewhat less than in the open market.

SPOTTING CURRENT TRENDS

At any given time, certain styles or trends of design are "hot." Research discussed so far has been about obtaining specific listings to use as a database for active job-hunting. The more comprehensive the database, the more obvious trends, or directions in your field, will become. While not all designers particularly want a "trendy" job, awareness of what is going on in the field—and where—increases your repertory and marketability. Since most firms get their best design fees when they capitalize on growing areas of design, they can afford to pay the best wages on these projects. Joining a firm in the early stages of work in a new area is beneficial because you enjoy startup enthusiasm and are a step ahead of the competition when the trend takes hold. For instance, if designers of health-care facilities and designers of multi-family housing find that design of assisted-living facilities (e.g. nursing homes) is increasing, and may offer more opportunities than, say, work in hospitals or apartment buildings, they may apply to offices doing this kind of work.

On the other hand, having a background in a highly specialized area may limit your clientele and job choices—especially in the public sector, where trends play little or no part in fund allocation, consultant retention, or contract award. Here, knowing *where* things are happening will be more important. If your expertise is in subway stations, you need to find out which cities are building new or renovating existing stations, not seek out national trends in mass transit. If your strength is in computer-generated walk-throughs of building interiors, you may be limited to firms with such specialized equipment and services, and trends will matter less.

The key, in other words, is to foresee future directions and tailor the knowledge to your own game plan.

Going right to the source can sometimes be the best form

of research. Firms performing a specialized type of work invariably know their competition. When applying to a firm that has no current job openings, ask which other firms are active in your area. Most would-be employers will open up if they feel they have nothing to lose. This process can be repeated any number of times until you have a satisfactory, if not comprehensive, list of possibilities.

THREE

OCCUPATIONS

Choose a job you love and you will never have to work a day in your life.   —Confucius (551–479 BCE)

Whatever the job you seek, understand it in detail. What are its ingredients? How do they work together? What are the end results? Making your way through the process of getting a job is a challenge. Designers who best grasp the challenge and follow it through are the most successful.

The main purpose of this chapter is to give you a broad understanding of the overall design job market. Many job seekers are unaware of the full range and far-reaching applicability of their talents and abilities. As professional versatility and flexibility become progressively more important in the marketplace, designers will have to keep pace. Those who can wear more than one hat will come out ahead.

RULE #6: BE FLEXIBLE.

One of the biggest challenges a designer confronts is orchestrating all the separate and essential aspects of a complicated building project. Teamwork is essential, so the better you understand the functions of the entire team, the broader the

realm of professional opportunities that will emerge; you may
have five potential job markets, instead of one.

OCCUPATIONS AND DESCRIPTIONS

This chapter describes the major occupations involved
with design and construction of the built environment, and
supporting services for them. They include:

architecture (including historic preservation);
interior design;
corporate design;
facilities planning and management;
planning and sitework;
graphic design and computer graphics;
construction and construction management;
surveying;
code analysis;
environmental and sustainable design;
manufacturer's representative;
law;
academia;
real estate development;
design-build;
internships and apprenticeships;
writing; and
other areas

None of these specialties is independent. The more experienced you are, the more areas of design will be on your radar,
giving you a greater understanding and appreciation of your
own area.

Architecture

Architecture as we know it, with its customary education, apprenticeship, and subsequent practice, dates only from the Renaissance. The AIA was not founded until 1857, and the first American architecture school opened in 1868. Before that, American architects were largely educated by apprenticeship, often abroad, and buildings were principally designed, if they were designed at all, by a master mason. He (sorry, not she) was a highly skilled artisan who supervised and coordinated other tradesmen, including the master carpenters, metal workers, and glaziers. Eventually the master mason became known as master builder, and then, architect.

The profession of architecture is now very broad, and growing broader. Most types of building design services, however, fall into one or more of the following categories:

> new construction and additions;
> renovation/rehabilitation;
> adaptive reuse; and
> historic preservation.

Historically, there has been an overabundance of professionals calling themselves architects, so some are forced to branch out into other areas of design. Moreover, clients are expecting more services from architects, so architects are offering more services in order to attract clients. Among these are:

Pre-design services
> potential site evaluation
> feasibility and preliminary studies
> programming
> establishing schedules and budgets
> zoning analysis

Design services
   surveying
   conceptual and schematic design
   design development
   working drawings/detailing
   technical specifications writing
   construction cost estimating
   code analysis and violations remediation
   value engineering and planning (VE)
Construction Services
   bidding
   building permit acquisition
   construction supervision
   submittal review
   RFI responses
   executing change orders
   punchlist and Certificate of Occupancy (C of O)
   contract review

When applying for an architectural position, it is best to use industry-accepted job titles to describe your past employment, even if they were not assigned to you at the time. These include:

   beginner, intermediate and senior designer/
      drafter/CAD operator;
   shop drawing checker;
   job captain;
   technical coordinator;
   project architect;
   project manager;
   specifications writer;
   cost estimator;
   field supervisor; and
   business developer/marketer.

Subgroups, such as detailers, renderers and model builders can also be mentioned in your application if they are areas of particular interest or strength.

Additionally, new internal (intra-office) assignments and functions include:

operations management
CAD management
technical support

Operations management is job tracking done throughout a project, used to determine where it stands relative to the pre-established budget and schedule. Operations managers record how many man-hours have been expended by a specific date on a particular phase of a project relative to the hours budgeted for the entire phase. This process helps to foresee and prevent cost overruns.

CAD management covers all computer design-related tasks; it includes installing and coordinating design software, setting office computer-design standards, plotting (and often assisting with) computer-drafting staff allocation and assignments. CAD managers keep abreast of software developments, and participate in training and manual writing. These responsibilities can be in addition to regular design tasks, especially in small-to-medium size offices; CAD managers are among the busiest people in the business.

Technical support departments, such as MIS (management information systems) and IT (information technology), the human backbone of all computer and electronic systems, most commonly are found at larger firms. Working closely with other departments, like operations and CAD management, they are responsible for the operation and maintenance of electronic equipment. This includes computers and peripherals, teledata, audio-visual components, and even security. If a computer, photocopier, or fax machine breaks down, tech support gets it back in service, and may also have input on new equipment purchases. In small offices, CAD management and tech support staff may be one and the same.

Interior Design

The independent profession of interior design is a post-World War II phenomenon. It has its own courses of study, and in some jurisdictions, principals in interior design firms must be certified. A building shell can only be constructed once, but interiors can be fit out and rebuilt any number of times, so it is no wonder the field is growing rapidly despite stringent professional requirements. More than a few architects have gotten their fingers in this pie and, I submit, the results are for the better.

Interior design is often the lead discipline in the team tackling a design assignment in an existing structure, including:

> programming;
> facilities planning and management;
> space planning;
> furnishing and fixture planning and design;
> lighting design;
> finish selection;
> specifications;
> purchasing;
> cost estimating; and
> construction supervision.

Interiors firms often act in multiple capacities, extending beyond design into merchandising—providing and installing furnishings, fixtures, and finishes. An interior designer may act as purchasing agent for a client. In this capacity, the designer acts as a middleman, who may buy, say, desks from the manufacturer or supplier and sell them to the client (usually at a profit). Or, the designer can opt to do it all. A turn-key residential interior, for example, is a job that includes all design and decorating services, all furnishings and fixtures, all finishes and, where applicable, architectural and other related work (e.g., millwork) at a quoted price. Design services can also be broken down separately from supply and installation costs. Almost any combination is possible, and job opportunities are numerous; job seekers with capabilities in both design and merchandising will go furthest.

Interior design teams have a project designer, handling all internal design-related tasks, and a project manager, handling client and contractor-related affairs; on smaller projects, one person may do both. Other positions include space planners, detailers, fixture, furnishing, and equipment (FF&E) specifiers, finish specifiers, and often, architects.

Corporate Design

There are as many areas of corporate design as there are industries—profit and non-profit, commercial and charitable, publicly and privately held—and therefore corporate design makes up one of the largest segments of the design job market. For our purposes, corporate design is defined as work performed in-house by designers employed by corporate groups. An individual segment of such design, facilities planning and management, is treated separately below.

In-house design departments employ a wide range of specialists: architects, engineers, interior designers, industrial designers, and lighting designers. A nearly endless and constantly expanding staff for particular business areas includes merchandise display specialists employed by retailers; clean-room designers for pharmaceuticals and high-tech manufacturers; clinical design for HMOs and hospitals; plant layout planners in energy and manufacturing companies; planning and development departments for universities.

In-house corporate groups rarely perform lead design roles in major projects such as company headquarters, large retailing centers, medical complexes, or manufacturing plants. Outside consultants generally do this work, especially in the case of new construction. However, planning, re-planning, equipping and refitting existing and new spaces are common in-house tasks. Corporate moves, departmental moves, upsizing, downsizing, and changes in the functions of spaces all require ongoing design input. Fortunately for designers, the scope of such services is broad.

Consultant Supervision

If a company retains an outside design consultant to, say, remodel a chain of storefronts, it may need an in-house designer to monitor the work and to maintain company standards. If a lender, such as a bank or an insurance company, wishes to verify that a construction borrower is spending its money wisely on a building project, it may assign in-house technical staff to track the project's progress, monitor payments, and verify aspects of it with legal implications (e.g., easements, rights-of-way, variances). These corporate employees then function as project manager, checker, quality assurance (a.k.a. TQM) officer, disbursing agent, and liaison with management. Corporate work is generally not as design-oriented as private practice. In-house design staff often do not physically see the projects in question. The corporate design office may be in New York, the project in a branch office in Illinois. However, corporate work frequently offers higher wages, better benefits, and increased job stability than private practice. Since the clientele is in-house, the likelihood of projects being funded and reaching fruition is somewhat greater than in a private design firm.

Facilities Planning and Management

Once considered ancillary to interior or corporate design, facilities planning and management (FPM) has come into its own. Businesses in the commercial, institutional, and public sectors may employ the FPM services of design consultants or in-house staff. Although some practitioners handle lab and research facilities, governmental buildings, or educational projects, most assignments involve corporate office interiors. Workstations, clusters, conference rooms, copier rooms, showrooms, and the like fill the program. Whatever their specialty, however, all facility planners and managers must respond to workaday needs. A cutting edge design response has emerged to provide speedy, yet flexible, solutions to new space requirements.

In cooperation with facility managers, *facility planners* start with given current and future manpower requirements for certain tasks, and establish a design program considering space requirements, FF&E needs, and necessary mechanical or electrical infrastructure. They perform space planning, fixture and furnishing selections, and layouts, and monitor the work of contractors, suppliers, and installers. Unlike some other roles in the design field, however, facility planners accept regular feedback from the client following completion of the project, so that work can be evaluated and fine-tuned if necessary. This is particularly useful to in-house design staffs, who may later take on other, similar projects.

Facility managers liaise with administration and facility planners, assist with manpower projections and accompanying facility requirements, determine who gets what equipment (e.g., desks, chairs, file cabinets, computers), and establish project schedules and budgets. Functioning as project managers, dealing with the needs of the physical plant, they also conduct periodic evaluations of facility usage, recommend revisions and upgrades, keep inventory, supervise purchasing, and make decisions regarding candidates for new design efforts. They do not generally get space-planning assignments. Some or all of this work may be performed in-house.

Planning and Sitework

All new construction begins with planning. The focus here is on the physical (design) planning—including urban and regional planning—and site planning. Urban and regional planning, often master-plan–oriented, generally considers the current and future needs of relatively large areas or multiple lots. Site planning deals with current needs at an individual lot or site, and may or may not be part of a master plan. Sitework consists of the improvements that must be made to a site in order to best provide for the structure to be built on it, based on its physical needs and characteristics. Sitework frequently starts with a big ditch.

Design planning takes up where social and economic planning and functional programming leave off. It can encompass numerous disciplines: architecture, landscape architecture, geotechnical, civil and structural engineering, and surveying. A typical scenario illustrating how the various trades come together for work on a project might go like this.

Assumption: a new office building with an underground parking garage is to be erected in an urban area on a site larger than the building footprint.

> The client has already established the program for the building, probably with input from the architect.
>
> The surveyor performs topographical, boundary and utility surveys, as well as locating adjacent structures, if any.
>
> The architect uses the survey to do building massing, orientation, and above- and below-ground plans.

The architect consults with a geotechnical engineer for foundation requirements (piles, footings, etc.) and with a structural engineer for the parking garage. The architect also consults, probably concurrently, with a civil engineer to determine surface grading and drainage and locate new below-grade utilities.

The landscape architect is called in to design plantings, pavements, site lighting, and miscellaneous site amenities (e.g., fountains).

These professionals work together closely, and their respective tasks will overlap.

Sitework comprises virtually everything but the building itself—although the building footprint, massing, orientation, and entry points establish many of the sitework parameters. If your interests extend beyond building shells and interiors, consider sitework as a potential job. It is challenging and interesting, and also somewhat less competitive. Sitework tasks may include:

surface site planning;
sub-grade planning;
roadways, driveways, and ramps;
circulative and decorative paving;
plantings;
site lighting and security (e.g., CCTV cameras);
underground ventilation; and
site amenities (e.g., benches, fountains).

Graphic Design and Computer Graphics

Graphic design is a rapidly growing branch of the building trades, and does not require new building construction. Graphic design projects include interior and exterior signage, directional indicators, and decorative visual features. The

Americans with Disabilities Act (ADA) requires comprehensive signage to be instituted nationwide, especially in public spaces and facilities—from Braille signage in elevators to disabled-driver spaces in car parks. Signage is often changed when some aspect of a building changes. All habitable structures require some sort of signage, even if just a street address number, and some require enough to warrant a separate part of the contract documents or a separate package of its own. Some designers specialize in graphics exclusively.

Graphic design generally encompasses two-dimensional elements, whether decorative or functional, such as a directional aid, transitional mood-setter, or space-defining feature. An architectural background is generally not required, but a good graphic designer understands proper location and placement of graphic elements, mounting surfaces, and hardware. In addition, the designer decides the materials, colors, textures, and styles (e.g., typeface and symbols), as well as electrical components for lit or variable-message signage (VMS), and weathering characteristics (for exterior applications).

Architectural computer graphics illustrate the completed building or site project during design, giving owners and funders a thorough feel for projects before a brick has been laid. CAD specialists transform the work of other design team members into a 3-D graphic experience that can be understood by both designers and clients. Exterior and interior views of virtually any desired angle are now possible with computers; the "fly-through" can be a major marketing tool for firms with large or high-end projects, and an aid during the construction. Expertise with software such as 3D Studio VIZ or Maya is a highly marketable qualification.

Construction and Construction Management

Construction is performed by the building contractor staff; construction management (CM) works for the owner in an administrative capacity, assuring that the project is built properly, on time, and within budget. CM has become a major player in the design-bid-build cycle of typical medium- and large-scale projects. Designers are employed in both construction and construction management—and often earn substantially more than their counterparts in design firms. They must, however, be ready to check their sensibilities at the door.

Construction contracting administrative staff, whether office or field-based, generally have architectural or engineering backgrounds. They function as liaison between the project design consultants, their employer, and the owner or CM. They are responsible for correctly interpreting contract documents, advising of errors and omissions, coordinating subcontractors, and overseeing submittals. Most office-bound staff will also make occasional visits to the job site, and attend meetings with the owner and the design consultant. If this sounds a lot like project management (without the design input), frequently it is. Like a design firm, a construction company also assigns a project manager to each job, usually someone with a solid, nuts-and-bolts technical background.

Since the 1980s, in response to owners' needs for greater project control and expedience, construction managers have become increasingly essential and influential. They act as owners' representatives and user advocates during the construction and design phases of a project, sometimes supplementing designers with technical decision-making such as value engineering and constructability input. Job-tracking programs, such as Primavera, are widely used by this group. If it's power (and bucks) you crave, and you don't mind the highly technical nature of the job, this may be the place for you. While you may not have much occasion to pull out the tracing paper and 6B pencil in a CM office, you will perform the tasks that keep a job on track:

scheduling (e.g., critical path method or CPM);
coordination (designers, contractors, owner);

cost estimating;

change orders;

dissemination of critical information to, and on behalf of, of all parties;

assuring contractual compliance;

approval of payments; and even

assistance with legal support and defense (e.g.
claims; extras).

A design background is an asset for a construction manager, who must be well prepared to interact with design consultants, deal with design-related issues, and appreciate the
rationale behind aspects of a design that could appear frivo-
lous, problematic, or just too expensive to a non-designer.

Program management (PM), a recent offshoot of construction management, uses owner reps to plan and administer
multi-part large and public building projects, addressing building tasks with an eye to shifts in socio-economic and market cli-
mates. While this effort is useful for programming and
phasing, it also helps to ensure that a project will not be outdated upon completion.

Surveying

Building surveying is generally required for all but new
"ground up" construction. This type of surveying, as opposed
to topographical, boundary, or utility surveying, is often performed by the design team.

If, for example, a client has retained a CAD drafting service to do hard-line working drawings for a building renovation
project, it may also ask that same consultant to do preparatory
surveys, facilitating the work for the subsequently assigned design staff.

Realtors and property managers occasionally use designers
to take measurements and draw up the existing layout of the

property prior to marketing, because many clients want to see the floor plan early on. Public agencies and corporate groups use it to establish a database of property holdings. This work may strike some design professionals as condescending, especially in the case of a small apartment or house, but it is increasingly farmed out, and can be a good source of short-term or freelance work. It can also lead to subsequent design commissions.

Building surveying is nitty-gritty work, but good experience for newcomers to the field.

Code Analysis

A building code analysis covers such basic preliminary considerations as:

> building occupancies;
> fire rating requirements;
> egress requirements; and
> OSHA and ADA requirements.

This may not sound like design work. As with many other tasks in the design cycle, however, it must be performed, and generally is performed by designers. Such analyses often play an early and significant role in the design of large, complex and public projects, particularly those including new construction or major renovation. The analysis is written, and can stand alone; it can also form part of a larger design brief, or appear as notes on drawings.

More complicated buildings have created more code requirements, triggering a need for assurance of a structure's safety, comfort, accessibility, and environmental soundness. Although some design firms still perform this work internally, and no designer should go through a career without some exposure to it, firms are increasingly turning to specialized sub-consultants to adequately analyze all the legal, physical requirements of their own projects. Hence, yet another new branch of the building industry.

Code consultants specialize in building analysis, often coupled with fire protection analysis and design. These firms command good fees but work on an as-needed basis, saving the client design firm money by eliminating the overhead, work-flow , and learning curve inherent in performing the analysis in-house. If you have a strong technical background and writing skills, you may find this work interesting and challenging. It is *not* bitter medicine.

A related area, and a growing industry niche, is the job of expediter. An expediter is generally someone who functions as middleman between a design firm and a public agency, usually a department that issues building permits. In preparation for construction, the design firm (architects/engineers) issues contract documents to the local building department or other construction-governing body for review and approval. As part of this process, the firm may retain the services of an expediter to assist in submitting, following up the review, and obtaining permits. Some firms have such staff in-house, but more commonly they hire an outside consultant who specializes in the procedure to help move the process along. Time is money and permit delays waste it. If there are problems, the expediter helps address them.

This practice is most common in big cities with big bureaucracies. Many expediters have technical backgrounds, and all are expected to be up on the latest developments regarding local zoning, codes, OSHA, ADA compliance, and, of course, processing-related paperwork.

If you like dealing with bureaucracy, this is a job for you. Unless the expediting firm performs other functions, however, you will have to leave your creative sensibilities behind—usually little or no design work is involved.

Environmental and Sustainable Design

Environmental science—a hot area and a big business unto it-self—performs analyses of water, air, and light quality as well as noise, odor, mold, and hazardous materials (hazmat) abatement. Although engineers and technicians usually perform such tasks, designers can make substantial contributions to environmental research, including:

> energy studies (e.g., solar, insulative);
> ambient studies (ventilation, thermal, light);
> material evaluation and selection; and
> remedial investigation and recommendation.

Energy studies generally try to minimize reliance on non-renewable fossil fuels, most often by utilizing passive solar energy design, taking into account building orientation, insulation, glazing, and shading. Active solar components consist of photo-voltaic and heat-gathering solar panels, together with their energy-storing support systems.

Ambient studies deal with indoor air and natural light quality, balancing natural and forced ventilation, heating, cooling, and humidity, and task and ambient lighting. Structures which respond automatically to these factors are called "smart buildings."

Whether by using renewable organic materials, or recyclable inorganic materials, building systems—including structural, finishes, and FF&E—can be designed to preserve the environment without adversely affecting cost or schedule—and owners will be impressed. This major growth area, material evaluation and selection, has been fostered by numerous special interest groups, with the U.S. Green Building Council (USGBC) and its Leadership in Energy and Environmental Design (LEED) program in the forefront. LEED certification (www.usgbc.org/leed) is a nice feather in the cap—and job qualification.

Remedial investigation (i.e., clean-up or hazmat abatement) is not design-oriented but is well suited to those interested in the environment and capable of performing detailed building surveys, especially as relates to asbestos and mold. Virtually all asbestos and mold-related work is done in existing structures, so familiarity with earlier building systems and techniques is important. Engineers can do this; so can architects. Some environmental remediation firms perform both analysis and physical removals and reconstruction. There are big bucks in hazmat abatement, and the seemingly endless supply of buildings and sites requiring it assures its future.

Manufacturer's Representative

Product manufacturers complete the owner-designer-contractor loop, and have become key players in building design and construction. Their representatives (reps), salespersons and/or technical specialists are the people designers call when they have questions about a product. Contractors contact reps when they are bidding on a project and need estimates from the specified manufacturer in order to assemble a complete bid package. Some reps perform quality-control inspections of their product's installation at the jobsite and performance assessments after completion. Reps also attend trade shows and give seminars and presentations on building products.

A typical scenario involving a manufacturer's rep and an architect might go as follows:

> 1. An architect needs to specify a sealant for a project, browses through a general construction catalog (e.g. *Sweet's*), and finds a sealant manufacturer whose product may be appropriate. The architect may also learn about the sealant

online, at a convention, product show, or technical presentation sponsored by a professional organization. But the technical data is minimal, so . . .

2. The architect contacts the manufacturer at the number listed in the catalog, and describes the project needs for sealant to the manufacturer's rep. They agree it's likely that the product will be appropriate for the job.

3. The rep sends the architect a more complete description of the sealant in question, and possible alternatives, for review. The architect may go through steps 1–3 with several manufacturers.

4. After reviewing the information, the architect contacts the preferred manufacturer's office, is referred to a local rep (who may also represent other manufacturers in non-competitive areas), and sets up a meeting.

5. At the meeting, the rep elaborates on the product and tries to persuade the architect to specify it in the contract documents. The architect commonly shows the rep some working drawings, and both take notes covering each other's interests.

The process can end here. Even if the architect is sold on a particular product, however, there may be more correspondence with the local product rep over a period of weeks or even months. When satisfied, the architect specifies the product in the contract documents; the rep may even assist with the wording of the technical specifications. (This last step is forbidden on public projects.)

The owner sends potential bidders copies of the contract bid documents, who in turn check them for sealant requirements. The general contractor (G.C.) bidder contacts a subcontractor who does sealant installation, for a price quote. The sub then contacts the sealant manufacturer for a material price quote, often speaking to the same rep who dealt with the architect. The sub includes the material quote in his material and labor quote, which he then furnishes to the G.C., who assembles all the individual quotes and puts together a bid package, which is submitted to the owner. Since there is so much interaction between manufacturers' reps and the design community, it is not surprising that many reps have design backgrounds themselves. Working as a manufacturer's rep permits a designer to focus on just a few areas of construction instead of a thousand. Reps are some of the sharpest and best-informed people in the business, and are always enthusiastic about the merits of their products, and well aware of the competition. If your interests are more towards the technical and back-end aspects of the design process, and you like meeting new people—and earning lucrative commissions—this is a branch of the field worth considering.

Law

Claim support and defense is big business nowadays, and designers with technical backgrounds can contribute substantially to the process of proving right and wrong where buildings are concerned. After all, who knows building codes best? Designers without law degrees cannot represent individuals or firms in court, but they may still assist attorneys with work concerning design liability and construction litigation, usually including case research and organization and analysis of the results. Some firms employ lawyers with technical backgrounds to oversee the non-lawyer support staff. Virtually anything relating to the design and/or construction of a building can be included in the scope of such work. For example, if a claim involving errors in design documents is brought against an owner by a contractor, the law firm will want someone technically qualified to review the contract documents, submittals, correspondence, minutes, and other materials to determine where the problems and responsibilities lie. Design expertise is also required in legal claims focusing on the analysis of building failure or collapse (forensics), and in hazmat health-related claims, where it is necessary to assign blame for the health problems of building occupants. Designers can and should perform these services.

Some law firms do this work in-house; others outsource the work. Some private design firms specialize in forensic work. Construction consultants, a fairly new specialty, are sometimes called in to assist with cases involving law firms, insurance companies, and banks. Their tasks may include administrative as well as technical aspects of a project.

The legal component of the construction industry historically has constituted a small portion of the design community. It is not aesthetically oriented, but can nonetheless prove interesting to design professionals who can sort, assimilate, deduce, and articulate concise conclusions from a mass of supporting data. Paralegal course work may be required to qualify for this type of position.

Academia

Design schools have much to offer career-wise. It is nearly impossible in most branches of the design profession to practice without the proper educational credentials; in some they are mandatory. Design educators have a tough and unique job. Their task is to make realistic, rational practitioners out of artists without destroying their creativity or drive. Who would spend four to six years studying design if told early on that he or she will spend the next five years doing stair and toilet details? Educators have the job of showing the way without discouraging their students.

Why is teaching a good career or career supplement for designers? It offers:

steady income and job stability;

free time to pursue other interests, such as professional practice;

little or no professional liability;

a built-in forum for exchange of ideas and information;

opportunities for specialized or non-profit study or
research;

the ability to develop a design rationale and philosophy; and

a platform from which to influence the next generation.

Finding a full-time university or college-level job without previous teaching experience is not easy; many design instructors, lecturers, and critics start out small by teaching a course part-time or as a graduate teaching assistant. If teaching for a living is your goal, be prepared to start out as an adjunct or guest lecturer/critic.

Good qualifications for an academic position include not only practical and teaching experience, but also:

demonstrable interpersonal, communication, and
organizational skills;

publication of designs or writings;

serious research in an up-and-coming aspect of
the field;

more than the minimum education required for an
area of expertise;

fluency in a foreign language; and

good references from your professors.

If you have particular expertise in one or more aspects of design, use it as your springboard (even if it is not in the area in which you want to teach). Virtually any teaching experience is better than none, and getting your foot in the door is critical to getting indoors for a rewarding career. Compensation should not be the deciding factor if you have the offer of a teaching job. Most part-time teachers are expected to supplement their income while they are teaching.

Look for job openings in school departmental offices, trade journals (commonly listed under Positions Vacant), and monthly or semi-monthly newsletters such as the *Chronicle Review* (published by the Chronicle of Higher Education, Washington, D.C.; www.chronicle.com/jobs), or *ACSA News* (from the Association of Collegiate Schools of Architecture, Washington, D.C.; www.acsa-arch.org). Professional organizations and licensing boards issue lists of schools with curricula meeting their requirements. Contact these directly to enquire about openings.

The principles of applying to schools are basically the same as those for positions in professional practice—the more resumes you send out, the better your chances of a response.

Real Estate Development

Involvement with the marketing and sales end of the construction industry may strike some designers as an inferior occupation. However, keep in mind that, especially with speculative construction, many clients have the leasing and/or sale of a building in mind when they commission it. Designers can assist in making a property as rentable or sellable as possible; they can even participate in renting or selling it. Their professional expertise includes the ability to:

> evaluate a potential building site (e.g., zoning, area, topography, utilities);
> assist with programming, conceptualizing, and envisioning the project;

represent and help potential buyers in evaluating properties, or perform physical surveys for plans, data sheets, and feasibility studies;

translate other people's design documents for a developer's evaluation;

understand and describe operations and maintenance requirements;

assist with financial evaluations and applications (e.g., to construction lenders); and

make early estimates of the costs of potential new construction or renovation.

Some developers maintain in-house design staffs, but these staffs tend to do more administrative work, such as putting together construction loan packages, monitoring and coordinating contractors and consultants, expediting the acquisition of building permits, establishing community relations, dealing with historic or landmark designations, or assisting property managers and realtors.

Design-Build

The major difference between design-build (also known as design/construct and single source responsibility) and the standard design-bid-build process is that the designer and the builder work as a team instead of being separate contractors of the owner. Although the concept of design-build has been around since the master masons, the practice was until recently limited to areas such as single-family residential and industrial plants. By the 1990s, due to increasing demands by owners for greater speed in the building process, design-build had entered most major markets, and is growing rapidly.

In addition to greater speed, the benefits and the by-products of this change in relationship include the following:

involvement of the builder immediately, instead of at the end of the design phase;

more designer involvement in the construction process, assuring greater design control and compliance, and fewer "unpleasant surprises" for the owner;

an accurate project cost can be ascertained earlier, thereby expediting funding for the project;

contract documents, and therefore design time and cost, can be simplified and reduced;

a significant reduction in the submittals and approvals process (except on some public projects);

an earlier and reduced work schedule, reducing construction cost inflation;

lower financing debt service for the owner, due to the reduced schedule; and

an end to the often-fractious relationships between designer, builder, and owner.

Until now, builders initiated most design/build arrangements, retaining either design consultants or in-house staff to perform design services. Most designers, particularly architects, have been indoctrinated to resist responsibility for the physical aspects of a project. This outdated attitude likely will give way to overall involvement in projects, with designers also functioning as contractors and the construction staff working for them. The result will be not only greater profits but also better design.

In the past, involvement in the physical aspects of the business was considered demeaning, as if the creative and aesthetic concerns would be compromised if all efforts were not concentrated on design. Old ways still die hard, and the profession is moving into the design-build realm with some trepidation. Historically, professional pride was the overwhelming reason for this anti-building attitude, but fear was also a major factor.

Consider the following:

- **Financial risk**: Builders generally have relatively large sums of their own money on the line; if they were unable to complete a project for the agreed-upon price, builders would lose considerably, and possibly default. Designers as a group have been averse to such risks, despite the potentially higher returns.

- **Fieldwork**: Regular site visits are required to properly monitor the progress of virtually all construction projects. Some designers enjoy such outings, but many don't want to be bothered. They know all too well that the drawings are full of errors, and do not wish to be confronted with them in person. Still more likely, designers dread leaving a comfortable climate-controlled office for a rainy, muddy, or dust-strewn construction site, only to encounter a large group of workmen, frequently including the owner or the rep, all asking non-stop urgent technical questions. The project never seems to look as he or she expected. Problems are always "the designer's fault." Who needs this?

- **Class-consciousness**: Designers, entranced with the mystique of their professions, tried to appeal to their clients, as opposed to those who would actually execute the work. They thought that if they remained "above" lowly physical labors, they could interact with the client on an equal footing. After all, designer prestige came mostly from client prestige.

Work overload: "I'm already working twenty-three and a half hours a day—how can I take on any more responsibility?" Designers have often failed to see the forest for the trees. The building—not the drawings, models, specs, or the computer-generated walk-through—is the end. All designers must know this. Sufficient energy and concern for back-end tasks have seldom been the rule. And that's where the big trouble starts. Designers should pay equal attention to all facets of a project. Nothing will take care of itself. But—contrary to common belief—there is time to do it all.

Indoctrination: From the first day of design school onwards, designers are exhorted repeatedly to "put good design first." The naive interpretation of this theory has tended to be somewhat narrow-minded. Good design is indeed important, but it should complement rather than compete with the equally critical but less "fun" job stages. Ironically, the relatively recent preoccupation with computer skills has contributed to a lack of pragmatic ability. Newcomers to the field should emerge from academic programs able to take on real life responsibilities. Apprenticeships are a step in the right direction, but why shouldn't recent graduates be trained to meet with clients? They do in other professions.

Let's face it—the largest part of a building project is not design, but construction. And in construction lies the greatest control and money.

Conclusion: Change in attitude and approach + overcoming of fear = more work, more control and more $.

Internships and Apprenticeships

Historically, time between completion of design school and professional licensure was called internship; interns worked for a licensed professional practitioner in order to acquire sufficient experience to qualify for their own license. Professional experience acquired prior to graduation, generally while in school, was considered apprenticeship. While these terms and situations have blurred somewhat in the last generation, the hands-on aspect remains the crux of both. And well it should— every potential employer will look for internships and apprenticeships in every novice's resume. It is common for designers to have both, and for employers to offer both.

Originally, an apprentice worked for a master in his studio. They paid for the privilege. Now they work for a firm while in school, for regular wages, usually as the result of an ongoing cooperation between a school and a design office. The granddaddy of the program is the University of Cincinnati, where the concept was invented in 1906, but many schools now offer apprenticeship (a.k.a. cooperatives), and it is even required by some schools for graduation. Tasks are highly varied, but generally speaking students are assigned work which requires little or no experience but will give them hands-on knowledge in some aspect of design.

Internships, on the other hand, are for graduates who are entering the field full-time. Licensure qualifications differ by state and by discipline, but most require a minimum of three years' work for a licensed professional in a discipline to be eligible to file applications and take exams. Licensure is required for architects to practice on their own in all fifty states and Washington, D.C. Interior design requires it in twenty-two states and D.C. This minimum period constitutes the internship, and it forms the basis of all subsequent career efforts. It also weeds out the unready. Accordingly, those who wish to make the most of it should pursue positions with firms with in-

tern development programs (IDPs). Most school career-coun-
seling staff know the local ones.

Writing

As George Eliot wrote, "It is never too late to be what you
might have been."

Trade-related writing is rarely something design professionals consider from the outset. An interest is developed over
time, frequently in response to other aspects of practice. After
all:

> Every designer cannot be a Wright or a Mies.
> Spending all day on CAD doesn't grab everyone.
> Critiquing finished buildings is more fun than
>   trudging through dusty works-in-progress.
> Monday to Friday, 9 to 5—not for me.

Whether it's spec writing, proposals, history books, reviews,
or fractal studies, writing can be a very real and attractive alter-
native to studio work. This aspect of the profession is virtually
never covered in design school; employers downplay it because
of its limited billing potential; and there is a general industry-
wide lack of interest in writing. How many office practitioners
get past their reference manuals and trade journals?

The reasons for writing are similar to the reasons for
teaching, and the goal is the same: to share your ideas and experience with a larger audience. Literally every aspect of the
profession is included: students, apprentices, interns, teachers, project managers—even clients. An attractive prospect?
Absolutely!

> **Getting Started:** Start small. Office newsletters,
>   trade organization bulletins, descriptive outlines
>   of current projects for marketing brochures, or

local newspaper blurbs are good introductions to the world of writing. If you want to try writing a book, be aware that publishers require detailed submissions and supporting materials before they will accept a manuscript. You will have to write a little for the privilege of writing a lot, including:

- A proposal. Include the reasons for writing the book, its current relevance, and the anticipated market.
- A detailed outline. A chapter-by-chapter, topic-by-topic listing with brief descriptions of each major heading. A general rule is that the outline will comprise 10 percent of the finished product.
- Biodata/resume. Relevant experience is critical; previous published writings should be included, but may not be essential.
- Peer referrals. Some publishers want a second opinion of your proposal from others in the field, and will ask you for leads; professionals knowledgeable in your area, or who have written themselves, are generally best.

Getting Published: Many publishers are not interested in design-related books. Don't bother with those oriented to fiction or bestsellers. Major career, technical, and trade publishing groups are best, and more names will come through them (and writer colleagues) in the process. When ready with your proposal, consider the following publishing houses:

- Career Press, Franklin Lakes, NJ; www.careerpress.com
- Elsevier/Architectural Press, Burlington, MA; www.elsevier.com/architecturalpress

- McGraw-Hill Professional Book Group, New York, NY; www.mcgraw-hill.com
- M.I.T. Press, Cambridge, MA; www.mitpress.org
- Princeton Architectural Press, New York, NY; www.papress.com
- Rizzoli, New York, NY; www.rizzoliusa.com
- Watson-Guptill Publications, New York, NY; www.watsonguptill.com
- John Wiley & Sons, New York, NY; www.wiley.com
- W. W. Norton & Company, New York, NY; www.wwnorton.com

Other Areas

If you have not found your professional niche in the categories covered here, take heart; there remain many others where designers can contribute. Among them are:

stage and set design;
exhibit planning and design;
model building;
presentation rendering;
computer animation (for video entertainment, websites, real estate offerings);
software design;
architectural photography; and
industrial design (product design for FF&E).

Most designers can function productively in areas other than their preferred or strong suit, and they will be enriched creatively and practically by such varied exposure. Architects can do interior design; interior designers can be facility planners; project managers can be construction managers; and all can teach or write. Very little of our built environment has not

had some form of design input, and the areas in which designers can contribute continue to grow and change. Design, good
and bad, is omnipresent. As a result, the breadth of potential
exposure available to any designer is enormous; take it.

FOUR

RESUMES AND PORTFOLIOS

"Designers should be educated, skillful with the pencil, instructed in geometry, know much history, have followed the philosophers with attention, understand music, have some knowledge of medicine, know the opinions of jurists and be acquainted with astronomy."

—Vitruvius (80 BCE–25 BCE), Roman
architect and engineer

Your resume may be the most important written document of your life, just as your portfolio may be its most important graphic document. Neither by itself will get you a job, but either can make or break your chances. Each should communicate information about you and your career with the least possible material.

RULE #7: KEEP IT CONCISE!

In addition to these two key tools, this chapter also deals with cover letters and other correspondence, professional references, job applications, and other paperwork.

Most employers require at least a resume and usually one or more other items as part of their screening process. *All* your job-hunting documentation should be ready at *all* times. Each of these items is covered individually in more detail below, but each should be considered as part of a whole, unified package.

WRITING RESUMES

The resume is the springboard for all professional job-hunting. The importance of accurately, clearly, and concisely conveying your experiences, skills, and goals cannot be overstated. Make your resume as long as necessary and keep it as short as possible. A potential employer has but a few minutes to read it, and must be kept interested. What will keep them reading?

> concision: A resume that quickly imparts a reasonable understanding of your qualifications.
> professionalism: A resume with recognizable terminology.
> clarity: A resume that is well formatted, easy to follow, and free of grammatical and spelling errors.
> directness; a resume that is neither arrogant nor overly self-effacing.

Writing a resume is a design assignment in itself; each job seeker will want to tailor his or her resume to best advantage. Standard resume formats (available in career books, on word processing programs like Microsoft Word, and through professional credential-writing services) are starting points, but I recommend designing your resume yourself.

At a minimum, your resume should include the following, in this order:

1. Header
  - Your name, e-mail address, mailing address, phone numbers (cell, daytime, and evening),

and fax. Obviously, if you do not want to be contacted at work, do not supply the number.

- Professional credentials, such as licenses, memberships, or a doctoral level degree (AIA, ASID, RA, CSI). Do not include the B.Arch. or NCARB.

2. **Professional experience**, in reverse chronological order:
   - Dates of employment.
   - Name of the firm.
   - Firm's location (city and state; country, if foreign).
   - A brief description of work performed and projects accomplished. Be specific; include project cost and size (sq. ft.) if applying for a senior or a construction-related position. Do not list apprentice jobs held while in school unless you are a recent graduate (see below).

3. **Professional education**, from the highest level of education list:
   - Dates of attendance
   - Name of the school
   - Degree(s) conferred
   - Course of study, if not clear
   - Honors received

4. **Professional Accomplishments** (if any)
   - Project awards received
   - Published work (preferably built)
   - Professional citations and awards received personally (not by your employer)
   - Authorship
   - Teaching experience or fellowships
   - Specialized studies and travel

- Special office recognition (e.g., Employee of the Month)
- Public appearances
5. **Professional licenses**
6. **Special skills**
   - Foreign languages
   - Computer proficiency
   - Expertise in particular types of design
7. **Memberships** in student or professional organizations, with offices held, if any. Only recent graduates should include student memberships.

Applicants interested in foreign assignments should also include their citizenship, if relevant, native language, and relevant passports or work visas. All U.S. citizens looking for work abroad should possess current U.S. passports.

Items which should *not* appear on a resume include:

career goals (save for cover letter and interview);
hobbies and recreational activities; these can be discussed during an interview if they come up;
date of birth;
race;
marital status;
sexual preference;
religious preference;
membership in non-professional societies and organizations;
professional references (these are furnished separately);
salary requirements; and
photos of you or your work.

When preparing a resume, start with the easy parts, such as the header, licenses and professional memberships. Before you write the narrative descriptions of previous jobs, make an itemized list of what you consider to be major projects and accomplishments at each, and number them in descending order of importance. (They do not have to be listed chronologically within a given job.) This list will help you compose the job descriptions. Use the same order as your itemized list, but do not number any entries on your resume.

RECENT GRADUATES

"Great, but what about experience?"

Numerous new designers have been asked this question repeatedly by interviewers, to their extreme frustration. Employers' obsession with hands-on experience to the exclusion of all else can make you wonder why you bothered with a long and rigorous education, mountainous debt, and loathsome summer and part-time jobs. Your grades were good; you were president of the school's chapter of the AIAS; your school projects are well-presented in your portfolio; you have great computer skills; what more can they ask?

Experience, experience, experience! Every design employer looks for it first on all resumes—full-time, permanent experience, often a few years' worth. Neither you, nor anyone else in your position, can offer this, so how do you get a foot in the door?

Answer: find common ground, a connection *other than* professional experience, which will catch the eye of a potential employer—**inside links**:

> **The school link:** Check your research records; has anyone you have met also attended your design school? School affiliation can greatly improve your chances with potential employers (indeed, some firms prefer graduates of certain schools).

To find school colleagues in the business: stay active with your alumni association, attend school-sponsored events, join local university clubs, if any, and peruse trade journals and newsletters for names of prominent classmates. You can even call your department chairperson or another faculty member for some recommendations.

The job link: If you had any type of professional job while in school, but do not wish to return to it now, call someone there, preferably a principal, and ask for leads. Your school-time employer may know someone to contact in your region, and voila . . . a new referral! If you know anyone who is involved in construction, even if not design-oriented, see if they work with any designers. Remember: names beget names.

The personal link: Tell friends and relatives you are job-hunting, and ask them to keep their ears open for possible prospects. Think about social and fraternal societies, political organizations, sports clubs, health clubs, and hobby associations—even church groups. They may think of a prospect then and there, or even make inquiries on your behalf, especially if their jobs entail meeting clients and outsiders. You can even offer to give relatives and close acquaintances copies of your resume, should the right opportunity present itself. (It also serves to keep their attention, at least fleetingly, on your plight.) A bonus: potential employers respect referrals by middle age and older friends and relatives more than they do those from youngsters. Juice them for all they are worth!

The goal is to entice potential employers by meeting more than just basic entry-level requirements. Every connection you may have with them should be played up on your resume and/or reference list. With inside links, you can raise a bottom-of-the-pile resume to the top, turn a stock cover letter into a standout, and a "cold call" into a "warm call."

CHANGING JOBS

If you currently have a job or are between jobs and wish to find another in the same or similar field, feature the following:

> work on projects in up-and-coming areas;
> specialized computer skills, especially new or sophisticated software;
> major projects worked on, and supervisory roles in them;
> flexibility and multitasking—your ability to switch from one assignment to another and handle multiple assignments at the same time;
> pre-design work capabilities, such as programming, scope-of-work, and man-hour budgeting;
> marketing/business development capabilities; and
> client interfacing and consultant coordination.

CHANGING CAREERS

If you wish to enter a design profession following a career in an unrelated field you may lack relevant experience and education; on your resume, highlight the skills you may bring in these areas:

personnel, time, and money management;

marketing;

computer, especially programming, scheduling, and graphics (e.g., Powerpoint and spreadsheets);

prior experience with clients in the design or construction fields, including volunteer work; and

legal know-how, especially that related to contracts and claims.

Volunteer work for non-profit groups can be a good way to get hands-on exposure to design practices, and a professional reference. Remember, design employers are artists at heart if not in practice, and usually want a similar orientation in their employees.

RESUME DESIGN

Outsized or otherwise unorthodox resumes are risky and I do not recommend them; they may backfire with conservative reviewers. The exception is for employers who may expect a visually unusual form such as design boutiques or graphics consultants.

The following sample resume is a guide, not an industry standard or universal format. Revise it to suit your individual situation, and review it to best highlight your professional skills relative to a specific position. Multiple-page resumes are acceptable, but brevity is recommended. Always keep resumes and attachments to standard 8½" x 11" paper size.

RESUME

JOHN A. DOE

100 Main Street
Anytown, NY 12345-7890
USA *(include only if applying for a foreign position)*

Tel. 123-456-7890 days
    123-654-0987 cell
Fax: 123-546-9870
E-mail: JAD5@aol.com

EXPERIENCE:

2002–Present **THE GLOBAL DESIGN GROUP, LLC**
Anytown, NY
Project manager and senior designer for the Domestic Design Division.
Projects include the $10 million American headquarters for the XYZ
Corporation, Townville, NY, and the renovation of the branch office of the
ZYX Company, Big City, TX. Responsibilities include programming, contract
documents, technical specifications, and cost estimating, as well as client
interfacing and man-hour budgeting.

1999–2002 **WILLIAMS & MARKS, PC**
Capital City, MA
Senior designer for the Northeast Design Department. Task Leader for the
interior planning and design of the H2O Company hydro-fluid facility,
Watertown, NE; Project Planner for the Domus Maison residential
development, Homedale, KY. Responsibilities included design documents,
scheduling and site surveying.

1997–1999 **BRUNELLESCHI & MADERNO, SA**
Hill Valley, FL
Designer for the Conceptual and Schematic Team. Assignments included CAD
drafting of design documents for the Typhoon Club, Boca Viento, FL, and
presentation boards for the Duomo Secular Center, Apmat, FL.

EDUCATION:

1992–1997 **LYCEE UNIVERSITY**
Ecole Heights, GA
B.Arch., 1997

1998 **COMPUTER CITY SCHOOL**
Mt. Ordinateur, MA
Certificate in Computer Drafting

ACCOMPLISHMENTS: Received Anytown Chapter AIA Merit Award, 2004; Won 1st prize in
ASID Student Photo Contest, 1996; Authored *Kudos for Post-Modern Revival,* NEW DESIGN
magazine, January 2007

LICENSE: Registered/Certified [Architect/ Interior Designer], New York and Massachusetts

MEMBERSHIP: AIA/ASID/CSI

SPECIAL SKILLS: Computer proficiency in AutoCad 2000 and 3D Studio VIZ; Primavera
CM program; Working knowledge of Italian and French

REFERENCES: Furnished upon request

JOHN A. DOE

100 Main Street	Tel. 123-456-7890 days
Anytown, NY 12345-7890	123-654-0987 cell
	Fax: 123-546-9870
	E-mail: JAD5@aol.com

EMPLOYERS

2002–Present: **VITRUVIUS & CALLICRATES ARCHITECTS**
Baton Rouge, LA

1999–2002: **THE GLOBAL DESIGN GROUP, LLC**
Anytown, NY

1997–1999: **WILLIAMS & MARKS, PC**
Capital City, MA

1995–1999: **BRUNELLESCHI, MADERNO & ASSOCIATES**
Hill Valley, FL

POSITIONS HELD

Associate in charge of marketing, Project Manager, Job Captain, Shop Drawing Checker, Design Detailer, Intermediate Space Planner, Senior CADD Operator, Cost Estimator, Proposal Writer.

PROJECT EXPERIENCE

Mid-rise corporate headquarters, commercial interiors, renovation (office and retail), adaptive reuse (conversion of industrial to gallery space), industrial plant design, millwork detailing, interior lighting design, site selection and evaluation.

EDUCATION

1990–1995 **LYCEE UNIVERSITY**
Ecole Heights, GA
B.Arch., 1993

1996 **COMPUTER CITY SCHOOL**
Mt. Ordinateur, MA
Certificate in Computer Drafting

LICENSE: Registered/Certified [Architect/Interior Designer], New York and Massachusetts

Short Form

If you have twenty years of experience and a four-page resume, a short form may be right for you. It serves as a "fat-free" introduction and lists only major items: employers, types of positions held, project experience by category, education and licenses. Employers will appreciate the effort you made to ease theirs, and will immediately know whether further review of your full-length resume is necessary. Do *not*, however, use short forms if you cannot cover the major bases on one page.

Print your finished resume, long or short, presentably (i.e., do not type it on a 1925 manual portable and then make mimeographed copies). Most inkjet and laser printers are adequate, but print a test copy to be sure the printing is clean and crisp. If using photocopies, do trial runs before ordering 200. Tinted, heavy or textured stationery, while classy, is not ordinarily worth the extra cost.

When your resume is ready for distribution, consult your list of potential employers. When sending resumes locally,

1) **Inquire:** Phone or e-mail the firm or check its Web site and find out to whom your resume should be addressed. If calling, do not ask to speak with that person—yet! With the name of a specific staff member, the resume will get to the right person sooner.

2) **Send:** Mail, fax, or e-mail the resume. A cover letter is not necessary, unless specifically requested. If mailing, use a number 10 (4⅛" x 9½") envelope with a typed, not a handwritten, address. When responding to a job ad, include a brief note (neatly handwritten is okay) citing the ad, publication, and date. If e-mailing or

faxing, include the same on the subject line or a cover sheet. Address all resumes to the attention of the contact person, or, if there is none, to the Human Resources department.

3) **Follow up:** Wait at least one week, preferably two, from the date sent, then call and ask to speak to the contact person. If there is none, ask for the Human Resources department. Small firms may not have separate personnel departments. Do not attempt to talk your way past a receptionist by claiming to be anyone you are not. Do not leave job inquiry messages on resume recipients' voice mail and expect to be called back; you can imagine the number of such calls they get. Call until you get the person live, introduce yourself as a job applicant, and ask if he or she has received your resume. If so, has the recipient had a chance to review it? Can you set up an appointment for an interview?

This call verifies that your resume has been received and gets it and your name to the top of the pile. A similar procedure can be followed with e-mail, but be prepared for no or slow responses. If after two weeks (three, if international) your resume is not acknowledged, send another.

For each resume sent, record:

name, street/e-mail/Web site address, telephone and fax numbers of the employer;
date the resume was mailed, faxed, etc. (and the method);
name of the recipient, if any;
position applied for;

origin and date of the job announcement, if any; and

result of the contact, such as an interview.

PORTFOLIO PREPARATION

If the purpose of your resume is to get you job interviews, the purpose of your portfolio is to show off your ability *at* interviews. The best approach depends on the type of design and level of the position being sought. A portfolio can consist of a few drawings, or photograph binders covered in Belgian linen, or CDs with animated fly-throughs, or a written report. While not every design job application requires a portfolio, it is always good to have work samples ready to show a potential employer; they will demonstrate your capabilities, and serve as a springboard for discussion at an interview. Your portfolio is evidence of your design sense and sensibility, and its preparation is a design process in itself; make it possible for an interviewer to see your talents and abilities in a short period with minimal effort. Remember, the entire interview will *not* be spent reviewing your work.

Decide what professional work best illustrates your knowledge, talents, and interests. This is not as easy as it may seem, and changes over time. Items which can be included are:

photographs of built work;

design and presentation drawings;

construction drawings;

professional writing (excerpts if more than a few pages);

CDs containing samples of the above; and

explanatory text (for all of the above).

Note that portfolios and work samples are not necessarily the same.

Portfolios are formal, assembled, annotated volumes (e.g., binders) with both graphic and written elements. They, along with writing samples, are brought along to interviews.

Work samples are generally graphic-only, usually photos or drawings, and are presented loose, or as an attachment to an application or resume in hard copy or electronic form. They can also be parts of portfolios. They are frequently furnished in advance of an interview. Writing samples, unless short, are rarely solicited in advance of an interview, unless the employer is located outside your region.

When responding to job ads or requests, keep the following in mind:

> If a job ad requests work samples in addition to your resume, keep them letter-sized (8½" x 11"), or as close to that as possible.
>
> Unless an ad stipulates that all work samples will be returned, assume they will not; do not submit originals unless certain of their return.
>
> If a potential employer requests your portfolio after reviewing your resume (a good sign!) be sure your work samples require little or no additional explanation, since you will not be present at the review.
>
> Include work consistent with the employer's business.
>
> Submit a variety of work to show your versatility.

Students and interns can show examples of senior-level school design projects, evidence of design-related research (e.g., dealings with recognized designers, consultants, and/or agencies), and special computer skills (e.g, walkthroughs).

Keep in mind that experience implies, but does not necessarily equate to built work. Many projects, particularly in the private sector, are designed but never built. Plenty of cutting-edge designers have lots of experience, but little to show for it.

PHOTOGRAPHS

Photographs are generally the best medium for conveying an understanding of a completed project; photos may also show three-dimensional models of projects that did not reach completion. Black-and-white or color prints are better than slides or other media requiring specialized equipment, unless specifically requested. Enlargements (8 x 10) are fine, but not a requirement (unless a photo assignment is sought). Keep the number of photos for each project in proportion to its relative scope. For example, do not show twenty photos of a $10,000 newsstand and six of a $1,000,000 summer house. Do not show one hundred photos of any project. If photos are in a binder, include brief explanatory text for each project preceding the photos, including: the project name, location, client, date completed, and cost (and be prepared to answer questions regarding actual cost-to-budget comparisons). You may include the names of consultants on the project, but do not list names of contractors or fabricators unless you are seeking such a position. Do not include design program, theory or other narrative with the hard data. Interviewers are unlikely to read it. Arrange photos in proper viewing order: start with an overview, such as a picture of the entire building in its surroundings, and follow with details of the project, such as interiors.

DRAWINGS

There are two types of drawings to assemble for your portfolio in preparation for interviews: **front-end** and **back-end**. Front-end drawings include programming diagrams, conceptual (that is, pre-schematic), schematic, and design development drawings, as well as 3-D renderings, colored elevations and site plans, and other presentation-quality graphics.

Back-end drawings consist mostly of construction contract drawings—that is, working drawings and CDs. These show the nuts and bolts of a project, and are usually the successor to design development. They include dimensioned, annotated plans, elevations, sections and details, as well as schedules, egress studies, code and zoning analyses, phasing diagrams, drawing lists, abbreviations lists, symbols legends, and general notes.

What you assemble should be consistent with the nature of the position for which you are applying. Depending on how specific the job description is and the type of work you have performed, it may be proper to feature both. As a rule (except for entry-level applicants), more specific is better.

> Do not assemble front end work for a back end position, or vice versa.
>
> Prepare finished work only, not sketches on tracing paper or progress prints.
>
> Do not include large drawings or boards—scan and reduce them. These can accompany photos of their respective built works in a binder.
>
> Include only work for which you are principally responsible.
>
> Be ready to answer questions about details such as materials and finishes.
>
> Do not include school projects, unless you are a recent graduate.

Most job openings are for back end positions (which includes the construction phase), because they comprise the bulk of the design process, and are the most labor-intensive.

Employers often have difficulty filling them with interested, qualified staff, and they are likely to pounce on anyone showing the slightest willingness to do this work.

Most important of all, **be prepared to do what you show**.

PROFESSIONAL WRITING

If your professional strengths include writing, or you are applying for a predominantly administrative position, writing samples are a valuable portfolio item. The most common items are:

> reports;
>
> proposals (ideally ones which were successful in getting the job);
>
> design briefs;
>
> technical specifications;
>
> program manuals;
>
> published articles; and
>
> custom software programs you designed.

Do *not* include unrelated or personal writings, even if published, or correspondence, memoranda, or announcements.

DISKS AND DIGITAL CONTENT

CDs, DVDs, flash drives, and other forms of data storage are a must for conveying proficiency in animation and some types of renderings, but they are not necessary for displaying most graphics such as plans and details. Only bring disks, laptops, or other equipment to an interview when there is no easier way to display your work and you have confirmed with the interviewer that the media you intend to bring will be conveniently readable by them. If you have a personal Web site that shows samples of your work, give your interviewer the link to access it before the interview, but also take along a hard copy of any material you can, just in case.

COVER LETTERS

To formally introduce yourself—and your resume—to a potential employer, a short (one page) cover letter is sometimes appropriate. A cover letter may be requested as part of a job application to help the employer narrow down the list of candidates to those consistent with the firm's needs and practices. Cover letters provide a means of evaluating your writing skills (including command of English as a second language), personality (without getting personal), and poise.

You *should* include a cover letter with a resume when:

it is requested by the employer;

your career goals are not obvious from your experience (recent graduates) or education (career changers);

you want to switch from one area of the profession to another;

you are following up a referral; or

a job ad requests information that does not appear on your resume, such as salary requirements, availability, or willingness to relocate.

Do include the following in a cover letter:

Introduction: Introduce yourself as a [type of designer], living in [location] and working in [location: skip this if not working]. If you are responding to an ad, mention the publication, date, and position sought (this info goes in the "Subject" box if e-mailing). If you have been referred by a mutual acquaintance, give the person's name and your relationship.

Body: Summarize your background in one paragraph; highlight your major accomplishments, especially recent ones. (If you have experience in multiple offices, simply state the aggregate number of years). If you are new to the field, include a brief and informal listing of career goals. Do not make up goals, or give wealth or fame as a goal (even if they are!).

Location: When applying for an out-of-town position, indicate your flexibility and willingness to relocate, and your availability, whether immediate or future.

Conclusion: Thank the recipient for his or her attention and consideration, and offer to furnish any other information required. If you know the firm's work, say why you like it. Include your phone number even though it is included in the resume, and close simply—no cute "Deconstructively yours"!

Avoid stating or implying that you are currently unemployed (working freelance is as good as being employed). Don't mention financial hardship, even if you need a job yesterday—it puts you in a poor bargaining position.

Do *not* include in a cover letter, unless specifically requested by the employer:

items listed on your resume, unless recent or high-profile;

your design philosophy (save for an interview);

excessive enthusiasm (do not describe yourself as a "hard-hitting player" or a "demanding leader"; "hard worker" or "fair supervisor" are okay);

salary requirements (if you must give numbers up front, indicate a safe range or a higher-than-the-minimum amount from which you can negotiate; see chapter six for more on this);

why you left your last job (if you are between jobs); or

criticism of past employers.

Cover letters and any other correspondence with potential employers are critical when needed, and must be carefully and thoughtfully written. Get a second opinion on your draft and have someone you trust proofread the final version. If you are not a native English speaker, have all letters and resumes reviewed and edited by someone who is. [*See opposite*]

While there are relatively few requirements for a good cover letter, it is nevertheless easy to write a bad one that will exasperate your reader. [*See following pages.*]

This letter is composed of excerpts from actual cover letters I have received. While an extreme case, it highlights some of the more common letter-writing gaffes—run-on sentences that try to say too much, touching on subjects without elaboration, and pretending to be something you are not.

100 Main Street
Anytown, NY 12345-7890

Mr. Andrew Disegno   March 15, 2008
Design Visions
162 Catfish Plaza
Baton Rouge, LA 70820

Dear Mr. Disegno:

I am writing in response to your ad for a Senior Designer in the Sunday, 4
March 2007 *New Orleans Spectator.* I am a registered architect with over six
years of design experience in a variety of projects, and am confident that I
can bring the right strengths to the position. My recent accomplishments include the successful completion of several medium-size projects, among
which are the Baton Rouge VFW Center and the Moss Bayou Clinic. In addition to design, I have performed other related tasks, such as programming,
scheduling and interdisciplinary coordination.

As part of graduate school, I studied in the Beaux Arts department of the
Ecole D'Art Americaine in Fontainebleau, France, where I was awarded the
Prix d'Eclaire for my study of Space and Light in Urban Design. My writing
skills are both technical and market-oriented. An article I authored, entitled
Kudos for Post-Modern Revival, was recently published in the January 2007 edi-
tion of NEW DESIGN magazine.

I am a team player, but am capable of working independently as well. Each
project brings new responsibilities and challenges, and I take them on with
enthusiasm and awareness. Your firm's work is impressive, and I would enjoy
being part of your team. Per your request, I have enclosed my resume and a
few recent work samples. I look forward to meeting with you.

Very truly yours,

Tod P. Vanderwaits

encl

100 Main Street
Anytown, NY 12345-7890

Mr. Andrew Disegno   March 15, 2008
Design Visions
162 Catfish Plaza
Baton Ruoge, LA 70820

Re: Resume

Dear Mr. Disegna,

If your firm is ready for a T-I-G-E-R T-E-A-M designer, then look no further. I am responding to your ad in last Thursday's *Spectator* for senior designer, and am seeking a challenging and fulfilling position as a member of your group. I have over six years experience in a wide variety of projects, including commercial, residential and institutional. My most recent projects include the Baton Rouge VFW Center and the Moss Bayou Clinic.

My career objection is to be a lead designer on a team, as well as represent the firm at meetings and presentations. I can wear several hats at once, and/but always give each role my best effort. I prefer front-end work, especially that which entails working closely with clients for programming and schematics, but will see a job through to the end.

Without getting into too many specifics (see resume), or risking *du veja,* I just wish to express my interest in your firm's work, and am confident that I can be of service. Also, I would ask that you waive the requirement for registration. For your edification, I have attached some samples of my work and my school transcripts.

Please respond as soon as possible, as time is of the essence. I look to meeting you, and for much happiness in years to come.

Sincerley,

Tod P. Vanderwaits

- *Mr. Disegno* (heading) / *Mr. Disegna* (salutation): Nothing will irritate your interviewers more than misspelling their names!

- *T-I-G-E-R T-E-A-M designer*: A display of conceit and recklessness.

- *My career objection*: Misuse of a word.

- . . . *lead designer on a team*: Not only is this *not* a career objective, but it implies that the applicant does not want to perform hands-on work.

- . . . *represent the firm at meetings*: Let the potential employer decide whom to delegate.

- *I prefer front-end work*: Sounds lazy and needlessly limits the range of positions. Avoid, unless the position desired is specific (e.g., cost estimator or spec writer).

- . . . *du veja*: Presumably a scrambled "dcja vu"? Avoid such affectations, especially if you don't write so good.

- . . . *waive the requirement for registration*: Forget it. With the number of resumes most employers receive from qualified applicants, why should they even consider one who is not?

- . . . *school transcripts*: Do not include this or any other credentials unless specifically requested in advance by the employer.

- . . . *time is of the essence*: A dead giveaway that you are out of work.

- . . . *much happiness in years to come*: Trite, and rings of a foreign tongue.

- *Sincerley*: Among the most common of typos. Always use spell check and a dictionary; spell check does not flag words that are misused.

- Avoid conglomerations of flatulent garrulity, esoteric cogitations and equivocating phraseology.

PROFESSIONAL REFERENCES

"That bum—I wouldn't hire him to shovel sand!" I actually overheard a supervisor barking this on the phone with another firm, which was calling to check the references of the "bum" in question. Don't list someone as a professional reference without checking with him or her first.

RULE #8: KNOW YOUR REFERENCES!

Choose someone in your field who can vouch for both your character and your professional competence, who has known you reasonably well for a year or more, is mature, intelligent, and discreet, and is stable (the call could come while your reference is suffering through the worst day of his or her life; keep moody colleagues off the list). Do not list someone half your age (unless you are 99). Entry-level and recent-graduate applicants understandably may not have professional references to list. If a potential employer requires references anyway, use one or more of the following:

> A professor at your school, preferably in your department; ideally someone who actively practices in the field. (But after you acquire some experience—say three years—avoid listing academic references unless requested or when applying for a teaching position.)
>
> An employer or supervisor at a job you held while in school; if the job was related to your professional studies, so much the better.
>
> An older friend, preferably a professional, such as a parent's peer who knows you.

Print your list of professional references with your name at the top but do not attach the sheet to your resume unless requested. The list should include the references' first and last name with title, if relevant (e.g. Hon.; Dr.), followed by any credentials, job title and location, and contact information, generally work phone number or e-mail address:

> John A. Doe, AIA
> Principal, ABC Architects (Anytown, NY)
> Tel. 123-456-7890
> jdoe@doearchitects.com

> Vitruvius Magnus, ASID
> Senior Associate, Callicrates Design Group (Latin-
> town, IA)
> Tel. 321-654-0987
> vitruvius@callicrates.com

> Jane Entwerfer, Ph.D.
> Vice President, Computer Design Research, Inc.
> (Carbon Valley, CA)
> Tel. 1-800-555-5555, Ext. 2969
> entwerfer@cdr.com

Try to list a variety of references; they should not all work in the same place or do the same thing. If you have many, it is acceptable—and occasionally helpful—to include one or more in other fields. For example, an architect might list an engineer; an interior designer might list an architect. These names should be kept at the end of the list. There is no ideal number of professional references, but, as with cover letters, they should fit on one page.

Employers may also send a written request for references directly to your previous employers, copying you. This is becoming more common due to the litigious nature of employer-employee relations, and the reluctance on the part of many firms to divulge personnel-related information over the phone.

PAPERWORK

Job applications may be mailed to you in response to a resume or query letter, or you may be able to fill them out online. Some employment agencies require you to fill out their own application forms before listing you as a candidate for placement. Usually, however, you will be asked to fill out an application in the office, immediately preceding an interview. This is boring; just do it. More on this in chapter five.

Any requests for written information, credentials, or any other form of documentation should be provided expeditiously, within 72 hours. Fax or e-mail the materials, if possible. The idea is to minimize confusion or forgetfulness on the employer's part, and to keep your resume, which already has a potential employer's attention, at the top of the pile—and fresh in his or her mind.

AFTER THE PAPERWORK

Upon completing the application process for one job, start on the next; the effort must be ongoing if you are serious about landing a new position. It is certainly possible to make a full-time job out of job-hunting. Don't forget to review the list of resumes and other items you have sent out and follow up with a phone call or e-mail. Employers generally need a minimum of one to two weeks to properly review an application.

Keep your daily agenda organized to make best use of your time. The most effective job-hunting is targeted, based in research. Find out where the work is, and go after it.

FIVE

THE INTERVIEW

"Put yourself on view. This brings your talents to light."
—Baltasar Gracián, *The Art of Worldly Wisdom*

Interviewer: "We need someone to do the programming, design drawings, working drawings, specifications, cost estimates, submittal review, and field supervision. We need someone who can work with other trades, the client, the contractor, and the construction manager, and keep them all in line. We need someone who can handle multiple projects at a time. We need someone who works fast. We need someone who knows AutoCad, Quark Express, Primavera, Microsoft Access, and HTML. If you speak Taiwanese and Arabic, that would be a plus. There is a lot of travel and overtime. Does this interest you?"

Job Applicant: (gulp) "Um, well, ah, oh, well, um . . . sure!"

While this dialogue may sound far-fetched, all of these needs are real. Job interviews are an opportunity for you to sell yourself, and attempting to sell your services to a potential employer is similar to selling them to a potential client. You must fulfill both of their wishes. This chapter addresses how to be at your best before, during, and after an interview.

Usually, interviews are make-or-break opportunities, so everyone should be in top form when attending them.

RULE #9: BE PREPARED.

WHY THE INTERVIEW AND HOW TO GET IT

The purpose of an interview is to establish your eligibility for a job. Getting the interview is critical. How do you reach the interview stage? There are three common methods:

1. submission of credentials
2. direct communication (e.g., telephone, e-mail)
3. professional referral

Accept all local interviews you are offered; doing them is valuable experience in itself. Turning down an interview for a less-than-ideal position is shortsighted, and you risk losing out on a better opportunity in the future. Besides, interviews can be surprising, and can yield angles you hadn't considered. Go!

SUBMISSION OF CREDENTIALS

Applying to large firms can be time-consuming: most have a multi-step selection process. If a firm has urgent staffing needs and has received relatively few resumes, they may simply call all of the applicants in for interviews. More commonly, however, resumes are sorted by the applicants' qualifications. Resumes may be circulated among the principals. Principals frequently have considerable autonomy; they have different professional responsibilities, needs, and interests, and different criteria for new employees. Communication among the staff is not perfect: In one instance I received a rejection letter, and a request to interview, from the same firm on the same day from different partners who knew nothing of the other's review or decision. You can occasionally use this phenomenon to your advantage, by sending resumes to different principals at the same firm instead of sending one to Human Resources. The catch: You must find out their names first.

Employers who solicit resumes cannot meet with everyone who applies (nor is every applicant qualified), so they form a short list of a few names for the given opening, and these candidates are called in. If none of the initial interviews yields an acceptable candidate, the list may be extended and more applicants called in. Don't count on an extension, though—your goal is to be at the top of the list and at the top of the resume pile! Every resume should be sent with the expectation of getting an interview.

DIRECT COMMUNICATION

E-mailing or telephoning a potential employer may be effective as a way of introducing yourself before submitting a resume or other credentials.

If e-mailing, always try to get the name or department of the recipient. Again, reviewing the firm's Web site can help with this; at least it will likely include a contact e-mail address. Be up front; type "job inquiry" or something similar in the subject line of your message. Keep your inquiry short, to about a paragraph. Make it clear that you are interested in an interview, but that you will be happy to furnish any information beforehand. You can attach your resume (a digitally scanned or jpeg attachment may work better than a file attachment).

Telephoning a potential employer to set up an interview may also be effective as a way of introducing yourself before submitting a resume or other credentials. If the person you wish to speak to is unavailable, too busy to talk, or has incoming calls screened by a receptionist in order to *avoid* taking calls from job applicants, and you are told to send a resume, try to get the name of the proper recipient. Then you can call again another day and ask for that person by name. Your success rate may even improve if you say you are following up a resume previously sent.

Employers generally respond to job seekers' telephone inquiries only when they need help urgently, so good timing is key if you are to make any headway over the phone. But be warned: If you reach just the person you wanted, he or she may resent that a job applicant has actually gotten through. (One assured me that his next official act would be to fire the person who referred me to him.) If you do call, here are some pointers for success:

> If a job want ad explicitly states "No calls," don't call, except to verify the firm's Web site, address or fax number. A receptionist can provide this information.
>
> Try calling between 9:30 and 10:00 a.m. or 4:00 and 5:00 p.m. (but do not limit yourself to these hours). Principals and senior staff frequently work long hours. After 5:00, the call screening staff may even have departed, leaving a clearer path to the person you wish to reach. If you have called several times only to reach a principal's assistant, try to make friends. You may get help.
>
> Always be calm and courteous. Be patient; even if you have been transferred four times, put on hold for five minutes, and cut off in the end, do

not lose your temper. Cool down, and try again later. Do not call when distracted, angry, or seriously under the weather—it will show.

When you reach the desired party, introduce yourself and state openly that you are inquiring about a job application. Never apologize or ask if it is a convenient time to talk. The time is never convenient, and speaking with applicants should be considered part of a personnel director's regular job duties (but do not suggest anything to this effect).

Be prepared: You need to explain your interests and experience concisely. Everyone's time is finite and valuable. Suggest setting up an appointment for an interview within a week.

Be articulate; this conversation is also a test of your oral skills. Starting sentences with "I'm like" doesn't cut it. Poor or non-native speakers may want to prepare and practice a short script.

REFERRALS

If you have "connections" at an office, you may be able to bypass the sorting process and land on top of the resumes-for-interviews pile. Networking works.

If you have been referred by a mutual acquaintance to a senior staffperson, mention it up front when you write or call; good introductions make good expediters. Do not depend on connections to do your work for you, however. Once you have a contact, your resume, portfolio, and interview count.

Speaking with personnel directors or interviewers can also yield other referrals. If you are not offered a particular job but think you came close, ask your interviewer for the names of counterparts in other firms.

DOING YOUR HOMEWORK

Getting a sense of a particular office's reputation, and what it is like to work there from official sources can be a challenge. A firm that commands good projects may not have a pleasant work atmosphere. Conversely, a firm with lower-end projects could have a great working environment.

If you have scheduled an interview with a firm you know little or nothing about, do some research to prepare. What type of work does the office do? How big is it? How is it structured? If this information isn't available on the firm's Web site, ask the interviewer, or even his or her assistant. In any case, try to speak to *someone* in the office before the interview. Or, use your networking activities to learn the inside scoop about a company.

SCHEDULING INTERVIEWS

Schedule interviews carefully, even if the employer wishes to meet with you immediately. You need time to do research, to check your portfolio and resume, and to fill out an application. However, if you are lucky enough to be asked to interview right away, you may have little time for preparation. That is why you should always have interview-related material ready to go.

Expect to spend at least a half hour interviewing for a lower-level position, and an hour for a middle- or upper-level one. Allow time for a "cushion" in case the interviewer is not immediately ready when you arrive, time to fill out a job application, and travel time. If you appear rushed or distracted, the interviewer may conclude that other concerns are more pressing to you than a position with the firm.

Give interviews top priority among your appointments. Do not:

try to wedge one in just because you will be in the same part of town that day and have a spare hour to kill.

schedule one after a root canal, or before an important current job meeting.

complain if the time is inconvenient or is rescheduled. Remember, the employer is the client, and you want the job.

The best times to interview are when an office is least likely to be overwhelmed with other tasks—early morning, lunchtime, and late afternoon. If, heaven forbid, you are called for an interview on a weekend, do it. It does not mean that you would be expected to work weekends: an interviewer who is too busy to meet during the week is probably doing both of you a favor by seeing you when he or she is free from distractions.

WHAT TO BRING

Go to an interview equipped with:

portfolio and work samples (photos, drawings, writings, disks);

the name, address, and telephone number of the interview location, and the day and time;

the name of the interviewer or person you are to ask for;

two spare copies of your resume (more if meeting with a group, as usual with corporate and government employers);

your list of professional references;

photocopies of any professional licenses you have listed on your resume;

a pad of paper and pen for taking notes.

Avoid outsized or cumbersome items, such as books, or complicated attachments.

Unless you are applying for a strictly administrative position, bring along representative *recent* work examples. Senior-level class projects are acceptable for interns. When you schedule the interview, ask what type of work the interviewer wants to see. Plan the timing: portfolio and other work review should take no more than *half* the interview time. If the appointment is for a half hour, do not bring samples which will take 25 minutes to show. If in doubt, rehearse first, preferably with a colleague. After several interviews, you will learn what samples work best.

Don't leave anything until the last minute. Keep your interview paraphernalia in the same place. Do photocopying, printing, or plotting in advance. Check timetables.

What you *should* do at the last minute is confirm the appointment. Most employers are conscientious enough to inform interviewees of schedule changes in advance, but it is appropriate to ensure you are expected.

DRESS FOR SUCCESS

Most employers will not expect to see you in designer clothes. Even if individuals in the arts as a group are noted— and occasionally notorious—for their flamboyant outfits, an interview is not the time to make a fashion statement. (Once you are employed, you may follow the office code, if there is any.) When applying for a job, dress on the conservative side, as if you were going to meet a client. Employers will form a first impression of your "big picture," so be sure all aspects of your appearance harmonize. Don't wear a tailored suit with flashy jewelry. Don't wear blue jeans. Remember that appearance includes personal hygiene, hair, fingernails, and even posture.

A business suit or trousers with a jacket and tie for men, and a skirt or pants suit or dress for women, are safe in most instances, and essential for marketing, management, and firms whose principal business is not design (e.g., product rep, corporate, real estate).

ON STAGE

Plan to arrive a few minutes early. If running more than ten minutes late, call ahead and say so. Unannounced tardiness implies poor organization and aloofness. Conversely, do not show up half an hour early and expect to be seen directly; no one will be ready for you.

You are now at the office, ready to knock 'em dead. Give the name of the interviewer; sometimes you will need to mention it at the front desk when signing in. If the office has a "Glory Gallery" displaying photos or drawings of current and past projects, take a look.

You may be asked to fill out an application. Although much of the information solicited on applications may seem invasive or irrelevant, it is best to complete the entire form, including non-required questions. Human nature being what it is, leaving an application question blank may cause an employer to wonder what you are trying to hide. If an interviewer asks you why you did not fill in a line, answer honestly. If asked the reason you left a previous job, fill it in. If you were involuntarily terminated without cause, it is acceptable to write "laid off due to lack of work." Employers know the score, many personally. Any time an interviewer provides special instructions for filling out an application, pay careful attention.

Applications invariably ask for professional experience, which can be frustrating if your interviewer is waiting impatiently for you to finish. You should always have a copy of the resume you have likely already submitted; fill in the names, addresses, dates, etc. of current and previous employers, and, where asked for a description of job duties, write "see resume".

When the interviewer appears, greet him or her pleasantly (even if you have been kept waiting) and look your interviewer in the eye. Give a firm, but not viselike, handshake, and, toughest of all, *smile!* Even if you have been previously announced by name, introduce yourself again. If you have kept the interviewer waiting, apologize without making a lot of excuses.

Wait for the interviewer to offer a seat and take it, after the interviewer sits. Place your interview materials where you can reach them without getting up.

Even if you are brimming over with enthusiasm (good!), let the interviewer set the pace and talk first. The more you can adapt to the interviewer's manner, the better the communication between you will be. Always remember your goals: to communicate your job skills concisely and to comprehend your interviewer's interests clearly.

> Don't:
> address the interviewer by his or her first name
>   (unless invited to do so) or pepper your answers
>   with "sirs" and "ma'ams."
> be flustered if interrupted mid-sentence.
> whip out a checklist (taking notes is acceptable).
>
> Do:
> if there are multiple interviewers, address all of
>   them, not just the one who last spoke.
> encourage discussion rather than giving mere an-
>   swers to questions.
> be a model of unflappable politeness, even if the
>   interviewer is not.

answer everything that is asked, even if it seems
irrelevant or silly.

be mindful of your gestures and expressions,
which contribute to the interviewer's impressions
of you.

avoid word tics (um, I mean, you know).

maintain eye contact with the person you are addressing.

Approach an interview as you would a design problem: start with the general and work your way up to the specific. Interviewers often break the ice by asking you to tell them "a little about yourself." Take this question seriously. The interviewer really wants to know:

why you are looking for a new job now;

what type of experience you have (very briefly);

what types of design work you particularly like;
and

a little about your design philosophy (how you approach a new project).

They don't care about your favorite color or sports team, or how many of your relatives went to Harvard. If you are a recent graduate, concentrate on any professional experiences you have had, even if volunteer, rather than your educational background.

Whatever the *real* reason, try not to give the impression of being there just because you need a new job, and the firm placed a job ad to which you responded. Now is the time to pull out anything good you have learned about the firm as a springboard for discussion to impress the interviewer. If nothing else, keep your eyes open when walking through the office, and listen carefully to the interviewer's early remarks to pick up cues.

If an interviewer begins by telling you a little about the firm, pay special attention.

Wait until the interviewer is finished to ask questions. Unless you are now certain that you have no interest in the job, make it clear that you are interested. Be consistently enthusiastic, even if you don't love everything you hear. No job is precisely what it seems to be at first.

If a firm asks whether you are willing to relocate, ask where the firm's other busy offices are before responding; this may help you learn "where the action is" currently, both nationally and internationally.

If the prospect of moving appeals to you, ask the interviewer to contact the other office on your behalf, or forward your resume. If you would consider relocation (especially for a good offer), say so. If you cannot or will not consider relocating, say that you cannot relocate at this time, but might in the future.

COVERING THE BASES

If your interviewer is unorganized, uncomfortable, or new at interviewing, you can help set the pace and direction. If the interviewer does not bring up a subject you consider important, bring it up yourself. Subjects you should cover include:

> **Job description.** The ad you responded to may or may not have included information about the nature of the vacant position(s). Regardless, ask your interviewer for his take on the specifics and responsibilities of the job in question. You may wish to ask specific questions such as, Does the position cover all aspects of the design process, or is it specific to one or a few? What types of projects would I work on?

Bring up your own interests if the interviewer does not touch on them. If, after further discussion, it becomes clear that this position is not right for you, ask if others are available, or may become available soon.

Workload. Design firms tend to hire sparingly, not taking on new staff until they are confident it will be worth their while. Nonetheless, especially if you are leaving one job for another, ask about the firm's current workload and staffing. Where will you fit in, if hired? What about project workload; if the office is busy now, what about next year? (You don't want to be leaving a job after ten years for one with an assurance of only six months.)

Job status. Always verify the status of a job being offered: Permanent or temporary? Full-time or part-time? Direct or contract employment? ("Permanent" and "full-time" are frequently confused. A permanent job can be part-time; a full-time job can be temporary.) Because of the relatively high cost of maintaining large numbers of permanent staff, employers, especially large and corporate firms, increasingly are hiring project-specific staff under the rubric of contract employment (CE). The client pays a fee—generally under 40 percent of the worker's wages—over and above the salary, to the employment contractor. There is little physical difference between permanent and contract assignments and work environments, but CE salaries are usually calculated hourly, not yearly.

Office structure. In large, corporate and public offices, employees usually have a job title, often numerically graded, with specific responsibilities, specific supervision, and specific subordinates. Smaller offices are less hierarchical, but all firms with more than two people distinguish among the staff and their responsibilities. How is the office organized? Does the position you seek have a job title? To whom does it report? If not entry-level, who and what does the position supervise? How are project teams set up? If the answers to these questions are not clear, do not despair. The organization may be flexible, or you may be expected to wear more than one hat.

Company policy. You may ask for a brief description of the employer's House Rules. What are the standard working hours? (9 to 5? 10 to 6? Flex time?) Is overtime expected; is it paid or not? Can you get compensatory time off in lieu of paid overtime? Facilities: open plan, cubicle, or office? Handicap accessibility (if applicable)?

Work methods. Firms work differently, according to their structure, type of work, and an employee's place in the hierarchy. (Lower level staff do back-of-house design tasks; more senior staff perform supervisory, technical, and operational tasks.) Questions to ask include: Does the firm design on computer or by hand? Are working drawings done on computer or by hand (or both)? What graphics, word-processing, and spreadsheet software does the office use? Is software training offered, or is proficiency a requirement? If you are applying for a specialized position (specifications writer, cost estimator, code analyst), verify office reference standards: CSI, Mean's, IBC.

Benefits. Most interviewers provide at least a brief rundown of benefits. Those required by law are social security, disability, and workman's compensation. Other benefits may include medical/dental coverage, life insurance, pension, and 401(k) plans. Vacation policy, holidays, sick and personal days are other benefits; while it is all right to ask a few questions, do not take up interviewers' time on these issues before you have an offer, especially if you are applying for an entry or lower-level position, unless you have a special need to know up front.

Wages. Important as it is, the subject of money—salary, remuneration, or compensation—should be left for last in the interview, because knowing more may affect your asking price. If an interviewer wants to discuss it early on, politely suggest pushing it back until you have a clearer understanding of the firm and the job. Interviewers generally won't volunteer a figure unless it is fixed (as in public-sector positions). Even though they will have a range in mind, interviewers ask how much you want, ever hopeful that your sights may be set lower. Be ready with a (negotiable) price or a range (of no more than 10% of the total salary). Most salaries are calculated on a yearly basis, so have this number ready, but know what it means at a monthly, weekly or hourly rate. Wages for entry- and lower-level staff are usually predetermined, but middle- and upper-level job applicants should think big and anticipate negotiation even if your asking price is acceptable. Do not expect an on-the-spot offer (more on this in chapter six).

Other topics. More experienced applicants may inquire about other aspects of a job, but should use discretion (e.g., leave for later if additional interviews are anticipated): "perks," such as professional organization dues, tuition assistance, parking privileges, company cars, and the like; availability of day care (rarely provided or subsidized by private firms); and support staff. If you are seeking an upper-level position you may inquire about clerical assistance. Do not ask about furnishings, fixtures, and office trappings unless you are at a very high level, and then not in a six-man office. Even in a larger firm, requesting office amenities does not assure getting them unless they are already part of company policy. For a reality check, ask for a tour of the office. Observe whether the office looks busy (assuming it is not lunchtime or after hours), the staff appears happy and enthusiastic, the work in progress looks interesting, the furnishings and fixtures look new or well kept, employees have their own offices or workstations.

SIZING UP A POTENTIAL EMPLOYER

Know what to ask and what to listen for at interviews. Buzzwords and glib talk can conceal unwelcome surprises for a newcomer to the firm. Be ready to "read between the lines" of innocuous-sounding phrases such as:

1. *You*: "How do you staff projects?"
Employer: "I like to run lean."

Translation A: This office is well organized and efficient.

Translation B: This office is chronically understaffed.

2. *You*: "What are your work hours?"
Employer: "Our work hours are flexible."

Translation A: Employees can make their own schedule, so long as their work is done properly, and on time.

Translation B: The workday is indefinite; employees may be called upon to work erratic or long hours, frequently without additional compensation.

3. *You*: "Your ad was not very specific; can you explain the responsibilities of the position?"
Employer: "The ad said 'intermediate designer,' but we could use someone to do technical coordination as well."

Translation A: Your qualifications are broad, and you may be considered for a wider position than what was stipulated.

Translation B: The employer wants someone to perform senior-level work for intermediate-level wages.

4. *Applicant for a senior position*: "How are your project groups organized?"
Employer: "We need someone to lead the design team; they will organize it."

Translation A: The project designer position is va-

cant, and whoever fills it will enjoy some autonomy.

Translation B: The employer wants to dissociate
from workaday design tasks to concentrate on
marketing and managing, and needs someone
else to run the design effort.

5. *You*: "Your ad described the position as trou-
bleshooting—what does that entail?"
Employer: "Reviewing, coordinating, and revising
CDs and specs."

Translation A: They want someone to do general
checking, and interdisciplinary coordination of
contract documents.

Translation B: A project has gone awry; someone
is needed to rescue it.

REVIEWING WORK SAMPLES

Portfolio review generally occurs in the second half of the interview. If the interviewer does not bring it up, it's okay to mention
it yourself. If you have several types of samples, describe them
and ask the interviewer what they would like to see first. Place
each item on the table or desk separately and gently. Let the interviewer view the samples at his or her own speed. Don't dwell
on one sample for long unless asked. Don't recite a lot of tedious facts about the project. Give the name, location, and completion date and your specific responsibility if you were a
member of a team. Let the interviewer ask for more details. Unless asked, do not mention construction or production costs. Always speak positively of the projects, even if they were dogs.
Concentrate on what you contributed or learned. Leave the
work samples out until the interview is over.

CONCLUDING THE INTERVIEW

By the end of an interview, you should have a clear understanding of the nature of the firm and the responsibilities of the position. If not, you may ask for a clarification or two, but don't request a comprehensive recap. Don't dwell on any one aspect of the discussion—especially money.

If you are asked about your availability, be aware that you are not expected to commit to a starting date until after an offer is made and accepted. If you are available right away, say so. If you have to quit a current job, state how much notice you need to give your current employer. Always give at least the minimum expected notice, so as not to burn bridges (some day you may want to return). Also, the interviewer will want to know if you are a person of integrity. Do not suggest that your availability will be based upon the amount of the offer, should you get one, or imply that you are waiting to hear from other potential employers before making a decision and committing to a starting date. As far as you and the interviewer are concerned, at this moment there is no competition. Ask the interviewer for his or her business card. Shake hands, look the interviewer in the eye, and thank him or her for seeing you. It was a pleasure to meet him/her/all of them. And smile!

ADDITIONAL INTERVIEWS

When you apply for a mid- or senior-level position and the stakes, financial or other, are high, you may be asked to return for additional interviews. This may mean you have made it onto a short list of applicants after the first round of interviewing, or that the firm wants an increased depth of questioning or participation by other interviewers; if you would be representing the firm, hiring may be done by committee. A hiring manager from another office of the firm may wish to meet with you, either locally or out-of-town. Or the interviewer forgot who you were or lost your resume. This is not as uncommon as you may think.

You may be called in for two, three, even four interviews (my record) for a particular position. Although it's inconvenient and may make responding to other job prospects more difficult, remain patient and enthusiastic. Treat all new interviewers as you did the first. Do not expect them to know your background; they may be from other departments or offices. The more interviews you attend, the more senior the interviewing staff will be. Your presentation must keep pace, yet stay consistent (except clothing: wear a different outfit to succeeding interviews!).

DINING OUT

Some corporate employers conduct job interviews over lunch. Lunch interviews are really about sales, with the parties attempting to sell each other on their mutual interests. While your interviewer-host is still interested in your professional capabilities, it is common to get acquainted with general discussion (even sports!). Some basic rules of decorum are: 1) Order after the interviewer to get some idea of the number of courses and appropriate choices; 2) order food that is easy to eat; 3) avoid food that has a strong smell, like garlic; 4) drink sparingly, even if the interviewer does not; and 5) act as though you enjoy everything.

You can talk about food and restaurant decor, and, naturally, professional interests. Money, however, is usually not on the agenda: do not bring up salary unless asked. If both parties are still interested after the meeting, an office interview may be planned.

INTERVIEWS WITH
HUMAN RESOURCES (HR)

Some larger firms have candidates meet with HR staff, whose job it is to screen for basic job requirements, such as the legal right to work, language literacy and fluency, physical and mental health, and basic qualifications. Unless there is a problem in these areas, a regular interview will then follow. HR can provide information about benefits, pensions, wages, and company policies. These meetings tend to be dry and peripheral, but they are also virtually stress-free.

FOLLOW-UP

If you win an offer at the interview you should respond promptly, preferably within a week. Meanwhile, contact your professional references and let them know who they can expect to hear from. Whether or not you leave with an offer, it is good to send a follow-up letter to interviewers thanking them for their time, and assuring them of your continuing interest in their firm. If you do not hear from the firm within a week following an interview, follow up with an e-mail to the interviewer. The firm may still be interviewing or making a decision. Don't appear impatient, press for a deadline, or try friendly extortion ("I have another job offer and I have to respond pronto; what is your verdict?"). If, soon after, you do indeed receive an acceptable job offer, congratulations! If not, go on to the next prospect. It's not over till it's over.

SIX

MONEY

"Lack of money is no obstacle. Lack of an idea is an obstacle."
—Ken Hakuta, *How to Create Your Own Fad*
and Make a Million Dollars

Designers work because they want to design. They work for someone *else* because they need to earn a living. While as a group we may dislike discussing money, it is as integral to our job search—and survival—as it is to anyone else. This chapter discusses personal financial planning, preparing a money checklist, and evaluating job offers.

PERSONAL FINANCIAL PLANNING

Designing your own financial strategy is the most time-consuming (and important) of the money-related tasks, but you don't need to be an accountant or estate planner to do it. The process of establishing current and future wage requirements should be completed before you interview. Start with a list of your fixed expenses. Using graph paper or a spreadsheet program, tabulate your monthly household expenses; see the following list for a suggested minimum. (Do *not* include medical insurance premiums and pension contributions; these are often paid, at least in part, by employers.) Total the individual expenses associated with each item, for an approximate total of your desired *base net income* (BNI).

Non-discretionary installment debt
- housing (mortgage or rent) including real estate tax, and maintenance
- tuition or tuition loan payments
- car payments
- insurance premiums (not including medical)
- utilities (electricity, telephone/internet, cable television, heating)

Discretionary Costs of Basics
- food and clothing
- gasoline (if you own a car)
- public transportation
- miscellaneous (dry-cleaning and laundry)

Non-essential goods and services
- dining out and entertainment
- luxury items (clothing, electronics, jewelry)
- home furnishings and appliances
- domestic help and housecleaning
- charitable contributions
- recreation (sports, vacations, club memberships) and hobbies

Job-related costs
- commuting costs
- books and supplies
- professional equipment (computer)
- accountant and legal fees (if any)
- professional memberships and subscriptions
- day care

You can stop at this point, but consider the following additional items, and estimate what you are spending on the following and average it out over the course of year:

Job-hunting costs
- career reference publications
- resume preparation
- portfolio preparation
- postage
- telephone and Internet access
- interview travel costs
- savings (optional but recommended). If you have been out of work on a regular basis in the past, accumulate a dedicated savings of at least six months' living expenses when you are employed.

Convert your base net income (BNI) to base gross wages (BGW), by estimating the amount of your federal, state, and local taxes and adding them to your BNI. Use the previous year's federal and state tax charts (available online at www.irs.gov), or consult an accountant. Include social security withholding.

Proceeds from sources other than your job (interest, dividends, annuities) should not be factored in, unless they constitute a major portion of your income. Consider them gravy. Your BGW is your benchmark for all wage considerations.

Use this list (see following page) as an example, and adjust per your actual costs. If $3,500 is your monthly BNI, and you are in the 30% overall tax bracket (federal, state, and local), you will have to multiply the above total by roughly 1.4 to establish your BGW. This results in a monthly BGW total of $4,900, or roughly $58,800 per year. *This is your starting point for all wage negotiation.*

As for job-hunting costs and savings, use discretion when including these in your BGW. Say your job-hunting costs aver-

Sample Monthly Household Expenses

Non-discretionary	$ Cost
Housing	1,200
Tuition/tuition loan	250
Car payment	250
Insurance	150
Utilities	100
Discretionary	
Food and clothing	500
Gasoline (non-commuting)	75
Public transportation (non-commuting)	25
Miscellaneous	100
Non-essential	
Dining out & entertainment	200
Luxury items	125
Home furnishings & appliances	150
Domestic help	0
Charitable contributions	50
Recreation & hobbies	100
Job costs	
Commuting (gas/public transportation)	100
Books and supplies	25
Professional equipment	75
Accounting & legal fees	0
Professional memberships & subscriptions	25
Day care	0
TOTAL	**$3,500**

age out to $50 per month, and you would like to save $250 per month. This results in a total of $3,600 per year pre-tax, or about $5,000 including tax (using the 1.4 multiplier); not inconsequential. While these are perfectly valid factors for inclusion in wage requirements, they should not have the negative effect of increasing your BGW to an unrealistic number.

QUICK CALCS

If calculating your BNI and BGW is not feasible or indicative, decide your new wage requirements by adding a percentage onto your current or previous earnings. If you are an entry-level applicant with no wage history to calculate from, get an idea of going rates before interviewing; try www.salary.com and www.bls.gov.

Consider the current rate of inflation. Say it is 3%. Most employees are not eligible for a pay increase for six months to a year after starting a new job. This means you will need to earn an additional 1½ to 3% above what you make now in order to come out even next year.

If you have received a raise recently, do not count it. If it has been almost a year since your last raise, factor in an assumed raise of, say, 4%, what you would receive if you stayed with your current employer. Already, it is clear that you will need to earn from 6½% to 9% more at your new job just to break even.

Example: You started your current job eighteen months ago, earning $40,000. You received a 4% raise six months ago, and will be eligible for another in six months. Current yearly earnings are $41,600. A new employer will not offer a raise until after one year; assume it will also be 4%. As a result, the new employer will have to offer the equivalent of a 6% (4% + 2%) increase after a year, just for you to break even. This equates to an increase of $2,500. If you add another 2% to allow for a change in tax brackets, you will have to add an additional

$830, for a total increase of $3,330. This equates to an 8% overall increase. Your new wage requirements, therefore, would be $44,930. Round it up to $45,000. You may also want to add on yet another 2 or 3% to give yourself some room to negotiate.

PREPARING A MONEY CHECKLIST

Now that you have estimated how much money you need to maintain your current lifestyle and established your base wage, look at the most important variables in employer offerings. Three types of employer-sponsored benefits will influence wage requirements: those paid by the employer; those shared by the employer and employee; and those paid by the employee (either pretax or after tax).

Any desired (or imposed) employee-paid benefits must be added to your base wage requirements. Usually the most important items are medical insurance and pension plans: how much will you have to contribute out-of-pocket towards each? Other items that can serve as general indicators of an employer's generosity and solvency include:

Medical
- What type of plan is offered—managed care, fee-for-services, etc.?
- Are office visits covered?
- Are pre-existing conditions covered?
- Are prescription medications and eyeglasses covered?
- Is mental health covered?
- Is there a dental plan?
- What is the employee's contribution to the premiums for individual coverage or with dependents?

- Can you choose to keep your current coverage, or use a spouse's plan?

Pension

- Does the employer have a pension plan and, if so, what type—401(k), pension funds, profit sharing?
- What is the level of employer contribution?
- Can employees contribute?
- When are employees vested?

Vacation and Personal Days

- Are there firm-wide standards?
- How are vacation days accrued?
- Can unused vacation be carried over to the following year?

Holidays

- How many are given? (Most U.S. firms offer eight to twelve; public employers may be more generous).

Sick Leave

- How many days are allowed?

Overtime

- Is overtime heavy, occasional, or infrequent?
- Is overtime paid and, if so, at what rate (e.g., straight time, time and a half?).
- If not paid, is comp time offered?

Bonuses

- Are bonuses offered, and who receives them? (Employees eligible for bonuses are often ineligible for overtime pay, and vice versa.)

Relocation Expenses

- If you are moving at an employer's request, verify what portion of your moving expenses will be reimbursed.

Sabbaticals (generally for full-time, college-level educators):

- How often—every seven years?
- For how long—one or two semesters?
- Are full wages payable?

If you have to pay a major benefit out-of-pocket, factor a 2 or 3% addition to your wage requirements. If you know you will have significant out-of-pocket costs (e.g., for medical insurance premiums or regular prescription medication) add them up and factor in a multiplier if they are after-tax. If you are in a 30% overall tax bracket, and have to pay $100 per month after taxes for medical insurance premiums, you need to earn an additional $143/month, or about $1,700 per year, to break even, so add this amount to your BGW.

EVALUATING JOB POSTINGS

When you study job ads, consider the nature of the position described, the level of experience required, and the wages, if mentioned.

If wages *are* included in the ad, all the better, but do not base your decision on whether to respond to an ad solely on salary stipulated unless it is drastically below your expectations. There may be room to maneuver.

Ads with a wide salary range—say, $36,760 to $48,290—are the sign of a large bureaucracy; the range covers all staff at a predetermined level. A new, inexperienced employee's wages are most commonly at or near the bottom.

Employment agencies often inflate their listings as a come-on. Hourly wages listed in their ads may indicate freelance or contract positions, very often with no benefits.

In most ads, however, wages are nowhere to be found. Why do so many ads state "Salary commensurate with experience" or "Competitive wages?" Answers:

The employer may be new to hiring, or fearful of
    paying too much.
The employer may want to review the resumes re-
    ceived before establishing a wage range. A
    good response may mean a buyer's market,
    and lower wages; a poor response may suggest
    a seller's market, and higher wages.
There may be openings for more than one posi-
    tion, even if not mentioned in the ad, and wages
    for them may vary.
The wages may be substandard.

What can you look for in an ad that will give some indication of what the job pays, if the firm's name is not mentioned?
Do not call the firm to inquire, or mention your wage requirements unless requested. Instead, consider:

Office address, especially in urban areas, can in-
    dicate solvency and status. The better the ad-
    dress, the more the office can afford to spend
    on overhead, and on wages.
Ads placed by out-of-town firms may indicate a
    local labor shortage, implying a seller's market
    on their end.
A company whose primary business is not design
    may offer better wages than design firms.
If the ad requires premium qualifications such as
    professional licenses, advanced degrees, or for-
    eign language proficiency, the employer may
    be willing to spend serious money.
If the ad is large, elaborate, or under a non-design
    heading (e.g., construction management), the
    employer is more likely to be a big firm, that can
    afford big bucks. Small ads with minimal job de-
    scription are usually the mark of a small office.

DISCUSSING MONEY AT INTERVIEWS

If the first words out of your mouth at an interview are "How much does it pay?" you have already lost the job; if an interviewer asks you early in the meeting "How much do you want?" you should seriously question whether this is the right place for you. Both imply a preoccupation with money—anathema in all job-hunting. It is best to leave money discussions until later (even if you *are* egotistical and greedy!). Get an idea of the office, the work, the position, and the benefits before you get to salary. A good interviewer will want essentially the same in reverse, while sizing you up. These discussions take time.

Let the interviewer bring up the subject. If he or she doesn't, it may indicate that future discussion is desired, a good sign. When it does come up, you have two choices: 1) Ask more questions, or 2) Give a number (or a range). If you are not satisfied with your understanding about office policies affecting money, you may ask for clarification. Do not belabor these points, especially for an entry or lower level position. Interviewers are not always up on the fine points of office policy and may not even be the persons responsible for the decision.

Have your requirements and calculations prepared beforehand. Most wage discussions take place at interviews, so you should be on your toes. If unsure of yourself, practice (in advance) with some sample numbers.

How Much Do You Want?

So, the interviewer has popped the question, without giving any indication as to the wage to be offered. You are ready with a number—your base wage, or bottom line. Say:

> "I am looking for something around $40,000."
> "I would consider something in the $40–42,000 range."

"I would like to earn $40,000."

Do not say:

"I'd like to make $41,716." (Round off to the near-
est $500.)
"How 'bout 40K?!"

If the interviewer continues to look at you and smiles, that
is a good sign. If the interviewer looks away and takes a deep
breath, it is not.

Some common interviewer responses, in order of desirabil-
ity, are as follows:

1. "That is within our range."
2. "I would consider that amount." This may indicate you are asking for the high end of the employer's range.
3. "That is a little more than we were expecting to
   spend." You are probably out of the employer's
   range, but neither of you should write the other
   off until the interviewing is concluded.
4. "That amount is outside the range for our staff
   at your level." The firm is highly structured, and
   will not exceed the cutoff (wage ceiling) for
   your position.
5. "That's too rich for our blood!" This is a dra-
   matic, but surprisingly common, response; forget
   it.

Some interviewers will not immediately respond. If asked
about your current or previous wages, be truthful: $36,000 =
"upper thirties;" $40,000 = "low forties." What you are making,
or at least made, is an important reference point for the interviewer; most will not offer less.

If an interviewer tells you that your wage requirements are too high, ask what wage the company had in mind. Most interviewers will give you an answer. If there is a big difference, the response may be simply, "Substantially less." If the number is low, do not wince or snicker.

RULE #10: BE REALISTIC.

Negotiating Wages

For negotiating to be productive, both sides have to want success. Wherever wage negotiations take place—at the interview or follow up over the phone—be ready to spar a little. Negotiating is learned on the job, but it doesn't guarantee you a better offer.

The time to start negotiations is *after* you have talked money. If you request $40,000 and the employer offers $30,000, you may not be able to maneuver; the gap is simply too big. If the offer is $35,000, there may be more room for negotiation. But no matter how desperate you are for a job, do not let on. Negotiate as if you have all the time in the world—it will pay off. If the money is a sticking point, ask if it is negotiable. Many employers will say "Probably not much," or "That is as high as we can go." If they are not interested in further financial discussion you probably won't get a split-the-difference counteroffer of $37,500. You may gain another $500 or $1,000. If they indicate willingness to talk, that is better, but the number probably will not increase much.

Most employers state the near limit of what they will spend up front. Don't expect them to come up more than 5 percent: many firms simply will not hire until they can fill a position with someone in their price range, regardless of prevailing wages or applicants' qualifications. Upper-level positions may remain vacant for extended periods. Wages at high-end firms and design boutiques can be unreasonably low because working for them is considered a privilege. And there's the myth that great designers live and breathe their work, and are not in it for the money.

You may not receive a firm job offer—or even a response to your suggested wages—at a first interview. Most employers take time to consider all the applicants and their wage requirements before making a decision. Some do this quickly, some are agonizingly slow. *Try not to rush the process*: it could earn you an unfavorable decision.

Being called for a follow-up interview is good sign that you have been shortlisted for a job. If wages have not yet been discussed, approach the subject at a second interview as you would have before. (It is unusual, but not unheard of, to attend two or more interviews without any discussion of wages.) If wages have been previously discussed but come up again, be consistent. Request the same wages that you asked for previously. Be prepared to commit yourself to a specific dollar amount; succeeding offers will probably not be higher than this number. Again, do not expect an on-the-spot offer.

EVALUATING JOB OFFERS

Job offers are usually made over the phone, and generally don't appear first in writing. (A follow-up letter should be sent to confirm the verbal offer and your acceptance of it, but this is a technicality.) Whatever the means, when you get an offer, you can accept it, reject it, ask for time to think about it, or try to negotiate it.

If an offer is low but you are interested in the job, ask if there is still a chance for some discussion of wages. (Do not ask, "Is that as high as you will go?" The answer will be yes. Do not ask, "That's too low—can you come up a bit?" The answer will always be no.) If there is, give a counteroffer. If your original asking price was $40,000 and the offer is for $36,000, try suggesting $38,000. If it doesn't work, you can still accept the lower offer, or you can still ask for a little more time to consider it.

COUNTEROFFERS

If you have two offers or a good offer from another firm, but would not mind staying at your current job, ask if your office would like to make a counteroffer. If they ask how much the other place is offering, do not make up a grand figure with the notion that you have nothing to lose; the likely result is no counteroffer. (Never conjure up an imaginary new job offer; you may find yourself out of work.) In any case, do not expect an employer to come back with a counteroffer more than 10 percent over another offer or your current wage. True or not, employers tend to think that everyone is replaceable, so it is generally safest to approach this type of negotiation gingerly. If you are going to go through with it, be fully prepared to take the lower offer or leave.

The interviews have gone well and offers are coming in . . . congratulations! You know now that your experience, education, and abilities are salable. Deciding which offers to accept is a holistic process. Consider each job situation: the type of work, working conditions, and wages. Consider the advantages and disadvantages of each. Which would be the best match for you? Sometimes it is helpful to compare offers on paper; include wages, benefits, and pension, as follows:

Assumption: You have three job offers, with comparable work responsibility and working conditions, They are referred to as Firms A, B, and C. The first two are nearby; C is a longer commute but offers higher wages. Your tax bracket is 30 percent.

Comparative Wage Evaluation

Firm A	$/Month Pretax	$/Month After Tax	$/Year
Yearly Gross Base Wages	—	—	35,000
Medical Insurance (company paid)	0	0	0
Employee Pension contribution (401(k))	100	70	(840)
Overtime (paid straight time; light; say 5%)	150	N/A	1,800
Other (tuition reimbursement; lump sum)	—	—	1,000
Commuting Costs	75	110	(1,320)
Total			$35,640

Firm B	$/Month Pretax	$/Month After Tax	$/Year
Yearly Gross Base Wages	—	—	37,000
Medical Insurance (company pays part)	100	70	(840)
Pension Contribution (company paid)	0	0	0
Overtime (not paid)	0	0	0
Other (possible bonus; estimated lump sum)	—	—	1,000
Commuting Costs	100	140	(1,680)
Total			$35,480

MONEY

Firm C	$/Month Pretax	$/Month After Tax	$/Year
Yearly Gross Base Wages	—	—	40,000
Medical Insurance (company pays part)	N/A	100	(1,200)
Pension (employer & employee each contribute)	70	50	(600)
Overtime (not paid)	0	0	0
Other (perk; club membership)	50	70	840
Commuting Costs	150	215	(2,580)
Total			$36,460

Even though the gross wages vary by up to 15 percent, in real dollars all three jobs are within 3 percent of one another. You may decide money is not a major factor.

Distance from home may be; but Firm A offers paid overtime. Did Firm A indicate you would work overtime? Overtime may change from year to year, so it is usually best not to rely on this exclusively as a make-or-break factor.

Firm A will defray tuition costs for professional-related courses you attend on your own time, a considerable savings. The firm does not, however, require you to take these courses, and will not reward you financially for their successful completion.

Firm B told you that employees at your level have received bonuses for the last few years, but they are not guaranteed, and will fluctuate based on the firm's profits. As with overtime, it is best not to rely on this.

Firm C pays the best, but does its slightly higher wage warrant the extra time and expense of commuting? Can your commuting costs be considered deductible?

There is no universal formula for weighing the pros and cons: your choice will be based on your particular circumstances.

CONTRACT EMPLOYMENT

It can be difficult to make a line-by-line comparison between a permanent job paid by year, and contract employment, ordinarily paid by the hour. Contract jobs generally have *no company-paid benefits,* since you will technically be working *for* an intermediary placement company, but *at* the office you are actually assigned to. Bonuses are rare. Some contract placement companies offer—but do not pay for—basic benefits (e.g., medical, pension); it is not uncommon to have no paid vacation, holidays, personal days, or sick leave. If you average 20 to 30 days of assorted leave per year, this can translate to substantially fewer paid work hours. For contract employment, it may be necessary to compensate for the lack of benefits and time off with a higher hourly rate than a comparable permanent job. For example, if you are in the 30% tax bracket and estimate that paid time off and benefits equate to 20% of your base net income requirements, you will have to earn nearly 30% more per hour than at the equivalent permanent job, just to break even.

When considering contract positions, always verify the number of hours in a standard workweek. While there is no industry standard, most employers require a 35 to 40 hour workweek for permanent employees. Most contract positions, however, are for 40-hour weeks. Why? It's all about the money. Employees paid by the hour, with no paid leave, will want to maximize their work time and their workday, especially if the job is short-term. Those on straight salary do not have this incentive. An advantage of contract employment is that it almost universally compensates overtime, at premium rates (time and a half). As with a permanent position, most interviewers and placement officers will project how much overtime you can expect as a contract employee. This type of position is a favorite among employers facing job crunches. As a result, there may be a lot of paid overtime—exhausting, but great for building bank accounts!

YOUR NEW WAGES

So, you have accepted an employer's wage offer. Usually, your new salary will be close enough to your previous earnings that your lifestyle will not change radically, unless you relocate, change businesses, or bring clients in with you—in which case it may change substantially.

Wages depend on labor supply and demand, economic climate, and employers' workloads. You may replace someone who retired or quit; you may possess a special talent that an employer lacks. In most cases, however, new design jobs will become available as employers' workloads increase. There will simply be more people in their offices performing the same type of work and earning the same kind of money. Don't expect big jumps in wages from job to job, and remember: there is almost always someone ready and willing to do what you do . . . for less.

Deciding how much you want to earn and negotiating it with potential employers can be the most difficult and painful aspect of a job search. It can be frustrating, infuriating, demoralizing, and insulting. Good negotiating can pay off, but the process is best taken as an enlightening and grueling challenge. Still, all experience, good or bad, is valuable.

Then where does money really fit in? Is it a blessing or a curse? Does it stifle or promote creativity? Do we design better when we are not concerned about paying the rent? Should employers stop spending so much on computers and so little on staff? Do we work for money, or would we do it anyway, because design is in our blood?

All of the above. Money is a good thing. We need it. We want it. We cannot design or build without it. But we want other things from a job as well—we want a customized, well-designed package, balanced with some combination of the important ingredients: the work, workplace, people, and personal life. We are, after all, spending what we earn on our personal lives, not our jobs, and they should be considered equally. Personal fulfillment comes from work, but also from other facets of life. Design, creativity, art—money may help us realize these things in the end, but they start elsewhere. It is up to us to fill in the middle.

SEVEN

RELOCATING FOR WORK

"Make hay where the sun shines."   —Proverb, paraphrased

Design has gone global, and we are now in the early stages of a global designer diaspora. Designers go where the work is; they can no longer afford to wait for it to come to them.

For our purposes, working out-of-town means working full-time, for six months or more, in a location too distant for commuting on a daily basis.

This chapter examines the logistics, conditions, and implications of moves within the country and abroad. Moving significantly affects your and your family's life, both professionally and privately. It involves change, which can be welcome, even if it entails temporary difficulties; or it can be a cause of major trauma, with lingering pains and regrets. Understanding and being able to deal with change, therefore, is key to dealing with the challenges and mixed feelings of moving.

What is new about globalization, the force increasing our need to move? American companies have always conducted business and had goods manufactured abroad. At home, Okies trekked to California to find agrarian work. Laborers sledged to Alaska to build a pipeline. And everyone who could spell *computer* flocked to Silicon Valley. They all wanted a piece of the action. Few professionals are willing to move without a sizable payoff: what draws us to the new frontier?

DOMESTIC BUSINESS TRENDS

In the past, when the United States was in a period of relative prosperity, with low inflation and steady economic growth, no one would have had to travel far to find a job. Now, regardless of economic conditions, we are moving more than ever. Job specialization is on the rise, and the labor pool is becoming more segmented, and geographically clustered. Domestically, specialized firms are doing work in fewer, but more concentrated, locales.

Yet, even with abundant work going on all around you, you may still find yourself out of the loop if your professional experience is different from local firms' current requirements or your computer skills don't match what the employers require. Upper-level professionals may price themselves out of the local job market. Large companies are no longer limiting their major offices to large cities and are leaving locations with high taxes, high costs-of-living, difficult commuting, and lower quality of life—all in order to save money. This trend will probably continue for years to come, and has helped create suburban clusters of "theme industries." Businesses in general are going more the route of the suburban campus than the urban highrise. Industrial parks are in. Look at electronics in Silicon Valley, or pharmaceutical plants in northern New Jersey. Even American automakers have spread their manufacturing operations from Detroit to the exurbs. New enterprises often set up near others in similar fields, since the labor and expertise are already there. One campus begets another, and entire regions expand (and contract) on the basis of a small group of industries. Design positions are relative latecomers to this suburban growth phenomenon, but firms want to be accessible to their potential clientele. Regional companies with in-house design departments, of course, want their staff at hand.

Nationally, service positions—including design—have replaced manufacturing as the main event. Today, the "hot" industries include communications, health care, and entertainment. In fifty years, it may be underwater housing, teletransport, and cybereducation. If designers wish to reap the benefits, they will have to match the dynamics, and follow the migration.

FOREIGN BUSINESS TRENDS

American entrepreneurs constantly seek and discover potential new international opportunities, and many require design support. If an American-owned company opens a new office or factory abroad, it needs designers and builders; if it buys a foreign enterprise, it may need additional design staff.

Illustrating this trend are some impressive statistics. A whopping 82 of the world's 150 largest global design firms are based in North America (*ENR, 257,* December 2006). They all pursue international commissions, because that's where the work is. And when an American firm gets a design commission abroad, it will set up an office nearby, in part to monitor it, but also to help get additional work abroad. They will need additional staff, too. If you want this work, you will have to move.

International firms are also going after—and getting—design work in the U.S. as never before. There is global competition for global work. The ambitious design professional needs not only flexibility and mobility but the ability to get used to new surroundings, culture, and work environment quickly.

RULE #11: BE ADAPTABLE.

OTHER FACTORS

Besides following trends, why would you look for work out-of-town?

Increased earnings. Where there is a local shortage of design and other technical services—in up-and-coming, energy-rich or sparsely populated regions—wages can be higher, or taxes lower.

Wanderlust. Here is a way to see another part of the country, or the world, at someone else's expense. A specific location may be more important than a specific type of work.

Desire to learn a foreign language. What better way than 24/7 immersion? Language can be a stepping stone to other ends; you may not wish to live in China permanently, but learning Mandarin can be a valuable job asset for establishing Sino-American partnerships back in the United States.

Accompanying a spouse. Your spouse or significant other has landed an out-of-town assignment and you want to find design work to go along.

Better job prospects: The market for designers with your skills in your region may be flooded or nonexistent. Or your skills may be routine here, but in demand elsewhere.

DOMESTIC ASSIGNMENTS

Small private firms offer the widest range of professional exposure and responsibilities, and may bring relatively rapid promotion. However, they may not afford competitive wages; the workload may be uneven, job stability tenuous, fringe benefits minimal, and relocation costs not fully recoverable. Accept such a job if you value variety of work, opportunities for self-determination, job flexibility, and an intimate work environment.

Large private firms have more defined positions. Wages will be higher, bonuses more likely, projects larger and more long-term. Benefits may be better, and relocation costs reimbursable. It will take longer to show an employer your best work, and you will spend more time on bureaucratic tasks. Promotion may be infrequent, and partnership less likely. Take this job if you want to gain professional status, work on larger and/or more prestigious projects, work in and with bigger groups, get better job security, receive better benefits, and earn more.

Corporate groups only offer work in areas of design related to their primary business, so work is more repetitive. But since your employer *is* your client, jobs are much more stable. Wages are likely to be higher and benefits generally good. This job provides an in-house clientele, and a large, diverse workplace.

Public agencies generally work farthest from true design; they oversee outside consulting groups or act as consultants themselves to other departments or agencies. Studies and reports are done in-house; policies, budgets, and scope-of-work are established internally. The work is steady, money fair to good, and benefits often superior. Consider a public job if you are in a public position currently, and want to move up (e.g., local to state, state to federal); you want to be on the client (giving) end, and manage others; you thrive in a large, bureaucratic, and political environment; or the private and corporate sectors are dead and you can't find anything else.

JOB SITUATIONS

If you are looking for or offered an out-of-town position, ask the firm (preferably the relevant office) whether, if the job is temporary, there is a possibility that it could become permanent? Does the employer have other offices you may be eligible to transfer to in the future?

Investigate the job market in the region you may want to move to. A good one will mean that if for any reason the job you take does not work out, other prospects may be available locally. If not, you may have to move again. Are you willing to take this risk?

What are employer expectations of design professionals in the region? Are they more or less rigorous than your own area? Are working conditions better or worse? Are company policies more or less employee-friendly? Work environments tend to be different in urban and rural settings.

COSTS OF RELOCATION

"You want *how* much to move the piano?"

There are a gazillion factors, both obvious and hidden, to consider when estimating the cost of a move. While no one can predict every last individual expense, good planning will minimize surprises. "Hard" costs are those directly related to the physical act of moving (like renting a truck or paying movers); large firms may cover all or part of these expenses. "Soft" costs, by-products of the move, include local cost-of-living differences and changes in personal and professional lifestyle. To compare cost-of-living differences, look at the most recent GSA list of "Per Diem Rates for Travel for the 48 Contiguous States" (available at www.gsa.gov—click on "Travel Resources/Per Diem Rates"—or from the Federal Information Center, PO Box 600, Cumberland, MD 21501).

Hard costs include physical transport, storage, and temporary accommodations. Moving may be done by a moving company or renting a vehicle to haul your stuff. Different types of moving services abound, many specializing in specific types of moves; they will give you an estimate. Prices vary based on the distance, location of pickup and drop-off, quantity and nature of the goods to be moved, how soon the move must occur, how much packing/unpacking you do yourself, whether interim storage is required, and whether moving crews must climb stairs.

If you must remove belongings from your current home but cannot use them on the other end immediately, you may have to rent storage space. Where will it be? How much will it cost? And will you have to pay to move things from storage to your new home?

If you do not have a new, permanent residence at the time of a permanent move, or must maintain two homes because of a temporary assignment, find out what temporary living space is available locally. What will it cost? Will it come furnished? Can you cook in or must you dine out? Will you have your own car, or will you have to rent one? Where will your family live?

Finally, check travel costs. What will it cost you (and your family) to get to the new location? If you have a car, should you drive it, or hire someone to ship it or drive it while you fly? Will you have to make one or more return visits to settle personal affairs?

Soft costs include cost-of-living differences. Will it cost more or less to live in the new locale? How do basic goods (food, clothing) and services (utilities, public transport) compare? What about local costs, such as car insurance, parking, commuting, education (if children attend private school), domestic help, and day care?

How will income taxes in the new location compare with the old? Property taxes? Local sales tax?

And last, what about non-essential goods and services, such as luxury items, dining out, club memberships, recreation, and entertainment?

WORKING ABROAD

An assignment in another country can entail both greater risks and greater rewards than one in another part of the U.S. The advantages of international assignments can depend in part on the type of employer, and whether the employer has any U.S. ties. When seeking foreign employment, where do you start— at home or abroad?

American Firms with Foreign Offices

Probably the most common means for an American designer to land a foreign assignment is to work for an American firm with international offices. The advantages of starting this way:

> It does not require traveling abroad to get the job.
> Office standards and working conditions are likely to be familiar.
> Income tax and other tax implications can be better explained up front.
> Job duties can be readily relayed and understood.
> You can meet easily with others in the firm who have previously relocated.
> Some of the staff will probably speak English.
> You may have the option to return to the U.S.

The disadvantages are relatively minor:

> Non-U.S. staff may be subject to some controls from the home office involving company policies, hiring, or promotions, for example.
> Projects and staffing may not be decided in-house.
> Slumps in the domestic market may adversely affect the foreign office.
> The home office may require special accountability and reporting.

Some U.S.-based multinational employers, especially corporate and design-related groups, recruit staff for foreign assignments without requiring prior domestic stints with their company. Strictly design firms frequently expect their employees to prove themselves in a domestic office first. In this case, it helps if you already know the necessary language(s), have other experience abroad, and possess the applicable passports and work visas.

Foreign Firms with U.S. Offices

Foreign-based firms with U.S. offices are the next best bet. Again, you will probably be interviewed and hired at home, though the hiring process may take longer.

Some advantages include the employer's appreciation of American socio-economic and cultural interests, assistance with income tax implications, and awareness of American working standards and conditions. Interviews are conducted in English.

Working in a domestic office of a foreign-owned firm may offer more potential for a reassignment abroad than does a U.S. firm with foreign offices. For instance, the foreign home office is generally the biggest and busiest, and may occasionally need additional staff from another office. Or a firm may want to expand by relocating a core group of current employees. If you are not sure about a foreign move, working domestically first with a foreign-based firm may be the right move. You will have news of goings-on in other offices, and a sampling of foreign culture, maybe even an opportunity to practice another language.

Foreign Firms Without U.S. Offices

At just about every step, searching for a job at a foreign company without an American office entails more time, effort, and expense. Occasionally, a foreign professional labor shortage will cause a foreign employer to recruit in the U.S., but this is a rare scenario. Except in the case of temporary or contract positions, it is nearly impossible to land a design assignment with an exclusively foreign employer without spending a lot of time in the employer's locale. Do not send resumes to a firm in another country out of the blue and expect to be called in for an interview, even if you are fluent in the country's language. The best you can expect, assuming you have no foreign contacts, is a polite response suggesting that you contact the office the next time you are in town.

If you decide to pursue a foreign assignment, be prepared to spend time abroad. Unless you are fluent in the country's language(s), obtain as much information as possible about your desired destination. Contact the nearest U.S. embassy or consulate office of the country for help. Once you are on the ground, however, the job search approach is much the same:

> Have an e-mail address, local telephone or fax number, and preferably a street address (a hotel is okay) where you can be reached.
>
> Check local professional publications and job ads.
>
> Check Web sites, call offices, get names and addresses, and ask for referrals.
>
> Visit local professional organizations and employment agency offices.
>
> Mail, e-mail, or drop off resumes.
>
> Call or e-mail again to follow up.

Finding a job in the most desirable countries to work, such as western Europe, can be a formidable challenge, especially if you don't know the local language. In any event, don't expect potential employers to defray travel or other job-hunting expenses or to offer wages commensurate with those in the U.S. for comparable positions.

FOREIGN ASSIGNMENTS

When seeking work abroad, you must demonstrate your talent and ambition; it may be even more important to promote your special skills. Designers with artistic talent are easier for most foreign employers to find than people who can do something the majority cannot, or will not, do. What can you do that is special and salable? Some capabilities that are prized by foreign employers include:

> specialized computer skills, especially for translating conceptual ideas to pragmatic 3D drawings and cybermodels for the benefit of clients
>
> knowledge of construction materials and methods, especially in metric
>
> fluency in the language of the client, if different from that of the firm
>
> ability to incorporate modern building systems into a local design vernacular
>
> ability to teach English to a firm's staff (this can be a big factor in Asia)
>
> willingness to accept low wages (you can always pursue more lucrative opportunities while working, but you will already be in the right place)

International positions are often on a contract or per-project basis, meaning that you are committing to a predetermined length of service—whether you like the job or not. Other possible foreign assignments include corporate, construction, and construction management. These, however, are less commonly found abroad unless you are already living there. They are more readily available through affiliations with multinational companies in the U.S.; check here first.

FOREIGN EMPLOYERS

Not all firms abroad hire foreigners directly, especially smaller firms. Large prestigious firms with larger projects maintain a certain level and duration of workload; conveniently, these firms also tend to favor outsider placement. While attractive for its stability, landing a public job right off the bat can be all but impossible. (There are public positions abroad with U.S. government agencies, most of which are civil service; apply directly to the respective agency.)

So, what realistic foreign opportunities are left? It can come down to a process of elimination. The *best* chances are with large private firms and with corporate work.

In most cases, a job with a private firm abroad will be just that—a job, with no extras included, although you may be eligible for government entitlements. (An exception is some foreign jobs in developing countries or areas with a technical labor shortage, which will often include a moving reimbursement package as an incentive.) If applying to a potential employer directly, be fully prepared to pay for most or all moving-related expenses yourself. Unsolicited private foreign placement is the riskiest of all foreign job situations, yet it can also offer some of the most fulfilling opportunities.

When applying for a private foreign assignment, be aware that local work customs may differ from those in the U.S. Consult *World Citizen's Guide* (www.worldcitizensguide.org), or *Executive Planet* (www.executiveplanet.com) for a rundown of what to expect. Examples of cultural differences in design may include:

> Designers may have to deal with builders from the outset (not unlike a design-build situation in the U.S., although the two groups remain separate).
> One firm, frequently out-of-town, may do nothing

but conceptual and schematic design, while another, usually local, acts as designer-of-record. This is often the case with U.S. design firms with projects in other countries.

Some countries (e.g., Japan) have mega-firms that design in all disciplines, build and manage all trades in-house, turnkey.

Some Asian countries subject the project to sanctioned religious monitoring (e.g., feng shui), which analyzes a building's propriety in terms of orientation, height, bulk, colors, textures, and overall harmonic "vibes."

If you are looking for a corporate foreign assignment it is usually best to start in the good old U.S.A. Read trade journals covering foreign corporate building projects and newspaper international business sections to find out which groups are expanding abroad and start a list of potential resume recipients. Contractors and CMs, large manufacturers (electronics, pharmaceuticals), and large service groups (communications, financial services) are among the largest foreign employers.

Call to find out which company offices handle job placement abroad. There may be more than one; one department may handle construction; another, facilities planning and management. Write down *all* the numbers, call the offices, get names, and send resumes. Always clearly state your interest in foreign placement. This process can take time; keep other avenues open.

Job vacancies abroad, particularly in desirable locales, are often advertised in-house before any external announcements are made or outsider interviews conducted. If the position remains vacant for a period of time, then applicants who are not with the company will be interviewed for it. One more reason to join an international company at home first!

ASSIGNMENT DURATION

Do you want a job that is short-term (under a year), long-term (over a year), or permanent (no term limit)? Decide before applying or interviewing; length of assignment will often be among the first items of discussion.

Short-term foreign assignments, relatively rare in the design community, are usually for back-end work during a crunch period. Except for housing, benefits and perks offered will be few, and payment is often hourly. Because of the trouble and expense of foreign placement, most employers offer assignments lasting a year or longer. It is not uncommon for such an assignment to last the duration of a particular project. Applicants for project-specific positions, however, should *not* expect additional assignments in the same location following the completion of the initial one. Entire offices, in fact, can be opened and closed solely for one commission. Regardless of duration, this type of assignment is temporary.

Permanent foreign assignments, generally not project-specific, are generally in established, permanent offices of a company. From a company standpoint, permanent employees are considered more flexible in their job assignments, and frequently are the overseers of temporary staff. A permanent position with a large multinational office may involve transfer—perhaps even back to a domestic office—as part of the company's efforts to keep up with shifts in the market. If this is of interest, be prepared to relocate more than once.

LOCATION, LOCATION, LOCATION

Job applicant: "I want to work in Paris!"
Interviewer: "We don't have an office in Paris."

Job applicant: "Then how about Rome?"
Interviewer: "We don't have an office in Rome."

Job applicant: "Well, where do you have foreign offices?"
Interviewer: "Bahrain and Kuala Lumpur."

Job applicant: "Are they near Rome?"

If you are determined to go abroad, be prepared to spend time in a place you have never been before. Western Europe, for example can be among the most difficult places to find work, because there is seldom a shortage of qualified local labor, continental unemployment is frequently high, employers can be severely penalized for terminating employees, and governments may impose restrictions on foreign labor on employers.

This doesn't mean that you should not apply for a job in Paris or Rome, but it does mean that the more flexible you are about your place of assignment, the more likely you are to get it. Find out where a potential international employer has its offices abroad and where its work is strongest. Do not expect an assignment in Europe with a firm whose overseas work is predominantly in South America.

RESOURCES

If you want to work abroad, read professional periodicals; they regularly announce what design firms have recently been awarded foreign building projects. *ENR* is a good source.

Books that focus on the subject include:

International Job Finder by Daniel Lauber (Planning Communications, 2002)

Work Worldwide by Nancy Mueller (Avalon Travel
   Publishing, 2000)
How to Get a Job in Europe by Cheryl Matherly
   and Robert Sanborn (Planning Communications,
   2003)

Employment Contractors and Agencies are best for engineering and infrastructural positions; some specialize in out-of-
town and foreign placement. Positions can be of all durations,
but are less commonly permanent. Consult *Contract Employment Weekly* (Kirkland, WA), www.ceweekly.com.

Useful Web sites:

   www.international-job-search.com
   www.iscworld.com
   www.overseasjob.com
   www.khl.com

In the 1970s and 80s the Middle East was the land of opportunity for designers. Where will the next wave of development be? Currency exchange rates, export/import balances,
political upheavals, and economic growth and shrinkage all
are factors. If China (including Hong Kong), Southeast Asia,
Eastern Europe (former Soviet bloc countries), and Ireland
are "hot" spots today, different opportunities may appear to-
morrow.

CULTURAL ADJUSTMENT

The U.S. is a nation of immigrants, and Americans are generally among the best at acclimating themselves to new surroundings. However, there will always be a period of professional and
personal adjustment. In order to minimize unwelcome surprises, and improve your chances of getting the job, investigate

in advance the customs of the country where you want to work. Talk to others who have already lived and worked there; check out the Country Background Notes on the U.S. Department of State Web site, www.state.gov. Seek answers to these questions:

Will business be conducted in another language? If so, can you learn it easily? If an assignment is for a year or less, it is advisable not to move to a place where business is conducted in a language with a long learning curve. Is local tutoring available?

What is the form of government? If the country is a secular democracy, rights and privileges of residents will be similar to those in the U.S. If not, there may be restrictions on civil liberties, religious practices, and public activities, and even censorship of publications and media you take for granted.

What are the customs of decorum? When meeting colleagues or clients do you shake hands, bow, or offer your business card? When you meet someone socially, do you shake hands, kiss, hug, or hand out cigars? Knowing and maintaining proper social graces around acquaintances makes a big difference, especially in Asia. Consult the useful guide at www.culturebriefings.com, or read Robert L. Kohl's *Survival Kit for Overseas Living* (Nicholas Brealey Publishing, 2001).

Are you ready to work from 9:00 AM to 1:00 PM and then from 4:00 PM to 8:00 PM each day? If not, stay away from Mediterranean and Latin American countries, where a long midday break may be customary. Do you prefer to have dinner at home with the family? Verify that this will be possible before accepting a position in

Japan. Do you want Saturdays and Sundays off? Weekends may be weekdays in some parts of the Middle East.

Can you enter and leave the country at will, or are special documents required (see Necessary Documentation, below)? Will you need a new wardrobe? Will you live in the local community or in a compound intended for expatriates (common in Asia, especially the Middle East)? Will you be able to drive a car easily and at will, or use public transportation? Have you any special health needs and can they be met?

Whether you are an Albanian from Albany or a Mainiac from Maine, when in Rome . . . . Accepting the differences is what will make work abroad an enjoyable, stimulating adventure.

LE MOOLA

Both the U.S. and foreign governments impose rules and regulations that significantly affect income taxes for those working abroad. For temporary assignments, most employers offer beneficial pay packages that conform to government requirements. For detailed information, consult the latest edition of these publications from the Government Printing Office: the Senate Committee on Finance's *Taxation of Americans Working Abroad* and Senate Committee on Foreign Relations's *U.S. Law Affecting Americans Living and Working Abroad.*

Be aware of the financial implications of a foreign assignment *before* you commit to one. Ask:

Are wages paid in dollars or another currency?
Fluctuations in exchange rates can significantly

affect your net at the time of conversion. Make sure your wages will be payable in a major, exchangeable hard currency.

Which country's tax laws govern? To get the tax advantages of a legal U.S. non-resident citizen, you may be required to be out of the U.S. for a certain period of time each year. If taxes are higher in your country of employment, will you receive some type of exemption, or do you require a higher base wage to compensate? Some jobs' wages are tax-free, or tax-abated over or under a certain amount (most common in the Middle East).

What is the local cost-of-living? The more desirable the locale, the higher the cost-of-living. Most design jobs in most countries are in or near cities, and even in poorer countries, urban cost-of-living can be considerably higher than in the rest of the country. If your wages are not commensurate with urban living, can you receive assistance with necessities such as housing and transportation? To evaluate differences in the cost-of-living, consult the U.S. Department of State publication that lists day rates reimbursable by the U.S. government for its employees abroad, and includes most world regions and cities, *Maximum Travel Per Diem Allowances for Foreign Areas*, (Section 925, Civilian Personnel Bulletin Number 197), at www.state.gov/travel.

Finally, be aware that moving costs will be higher than domestic long-distance moves.

NECESSARY DOCUMENTATION

Legal documents needed to work abroad vary, but as a minimum, you must have a current valid passport as well as your birth certificate, marriage certificate (especially if your spouse also wants to work), and visa, Green Cards and naturalization papers (for U.S. immigrants). Keep these at hand to furnish upon request. (Do not attach copies of them to resumes or applications.)

Work visas, issued by the government of the foreign country, are commonly required; other types of visa usually do not permit, and frequently prohibit, working in the country of issuance. Do not apply for a work permit or Social Security equivalent until instructed by a potential employer or placement service. Employers who regularly hire staff for foreign placement can tell you what to expect for required documentation, and assist you in obtaining it.

Your candidacy for a foreign job may depend on your eligibility for the appropriate documentation. If you are not a U.S. citizen, and are applying in the U.S. for a foreign job, mention this immediately; the required documentation may be different from that of a citizen. Be aware of the rights associated with certain foreign countries by agreement: for example, the U.S. offers dual citizenship with several countries of the European Union (E.U.), including the U.K., Ireland, and Italy. If your heritage can be traced to any of these countries, you may be eligible to apply for a passport from one or more of them. Contact the embassy or consulate of the country in question, or inquire at the U.S. Department of State—and be prepared for a lot of paperwork.

If you already have legal documents from another country, it is easier to apply directly to an international company, and you'll have a better chance of getting work there. Do not fret, however, if you do not possess such documents. Most foreign employers assume that you don't and will make whatever special arrangements necessary to place people in their offices abroad. Their incentive to do so is strong if they need you.

SPECIAL AGREEMENTS

We all have the same basic living needs to meet in any location: housing, food, clothing, medical attention, and transportation are givens. If you have a family, you must also consider education, day care, and possibly a job for your spouse. You want a quality of life comparable to what you are leaving. Getting a written agreement is a necessity with out-of-town assignments, be they domestic or international, no matter their duration, especially if you are leaving one job for another.

Written agreements should be tailored to your individual needs; they can be one-page letters or lengthy legalese boilerplate, or they may be covered by company policy booklets explaining benefits, leave, and insurance. Regardless of form, they are binding. For foreign assignments, insist on a comprehensive agreement, including:

approximate starting date;

duration of employ, minimum or fixed duration;

job title and general duties;

pay: starting base salary, overtime policies, incremental increases, and bonuses payable;

health and pension benefits and contributions;

specially-negotiated terms such as extra vacation, flexible working hours, terms for working at home, perks, sabbaticals, home leave;

housing provisions or allowance, temporary or permanent (if temporary, for how long?);

transportation (will a dedicated company car be provided, an allowance for local commuting costs, paid-for travel to and from the U.S.?);

job for spouse (will the company provide or assist
in finding one, or with any necessary legal documentation?);
child care (company-provided or paid day care
for young children; good local public schools, or
employer–paid private schooling?); and
relocation (will the employer pay all or part of the
cost of the move? If the assignment is temporary, will return moving costs be paid?).

Always review agreements and other papers requiring sig-
natures carefully before you sign, whether they are forms or
tailored for you. If anything is unsatisfactory or unclear, deal
with it before signing. If the paperwork is complicated, a review by an attorney may be in order. Any agreement should be
in your language, or translated at the employer's expense by a
reputable service (e.g., Berlitz).

NEW IMPRESSIONS

So, you have decided to move. While the prospect of a new life
in a new place is exciting, the physical acts of moving and getting settled into new digs are arduous at best and traumatic at
worst. Those with families should realize that everyone in the
household will not necessarily adjust at the same rate. One family member's cultural adventure may be another's nightmare.
Learning the ropes at a new job may, at least temporarily, oc-
cupy you at the expense of your personal life, especially if you
are faced with learning a new language. Getting children
signed up and ready for a new school and violin lessons will take
time and attention. The roof and the sink may leak. Appliances
you took along may not work with the local voltage. Fido may
bark non-stop (or be missed due to quarantine isolation).
Remember rule #9: be prepared! And *bon voyage!*

EIGHT

STARTING A NEW JOB

"We're supposed to be perfect our first day on the job and then show constant improvement."

—Ed Vargo, Major League baseball umpire

PREPARING FOR A NEW JOB

The worst of it is over. The offers are coming in. They may be good or they may be barely above minimum wage, but accept one you will. If you are fortunate enough to have multiple job offers, great! The next step is deciding which one to accept. If you have received only one, this decision is, of course, eliminated. Whether or not you are currently working, the transitional period before starting a new job can be one of considerable elation, anxiety, or both. Either way, there are still questions to address and loose ends to tie up.

COMPLETING NEGOTIATIONS AND AGREEMENTS

Discussions regarding job assignments, wages, benefits, perks and, if they apply, moving-related issues should be concluded.

If there are outstanding items to be decided with a potential employer, or any questions or comments about a written agreement, resolve them before accepting an offer. Assuming the interviewing is completed, these can usually be taken care of by telephone. In preparation, make a short list of the topics in question, in descending order of importance. If you do not get past the first item, the remaining ones may not matter. Do not give notice to a current employer until you accept the terms of your assignment with the new one.

After you accept an offer, ask if there is anything you can do relative to the new job before starting. Filling out benefit and tax withholding forms, reviewing office materials, or job-related research can begin in advance. It is never too early to get a jump on the new competition.

GIVING NOTICE

Most design firms hire when they are busy, and do not want to wait long for new employees to start. If you are changing jobs, you will want to give notice based on what is least disruptive to your present employer, while also meeting the new employer's staffing needs. Two weeks' notice is generally adequate for all but the most senior-level staff, and sometimes less will suffice.

Before giving a specific end date, however, consult in your current firm's personnel department, in order to avoid snags. Make sure that:

> You abide by any minimum-notice period to qualify for collecting unused vacation or sick leave pay;
> If you are three weeks away from being vested in the firm's pension plan, you can stick it out;
> If your departure coincides with the end of your firm's fiscal year, you will not lose out on your

> profit sharing or pension contribution for the year;
>
> If you are due a bonus, staying a few extra weeks will allow you to collect it (this is most common at year end);
>
> If you are not starting a new job immediately, can you extend current medical coverage (e.g. CO-BRA)?

and so on. Stay active and interested in your current job until you leave.

SETTING A STARTING DATE

If you are not currently employed, setting a starting date can be as easy as exclaiming, "Yesterday!" If you are currently working, remember that giving an end date to a current employer and a starting date to a new employer are two different things. Quitting your current job on Friday doesn't mean you have to start the new one on Monday. Consider what you might want to do with time between jobs:

> **Travel.** You have not taken a recreational trip in two years; another may not be possible for a while. Now is your chance to visit Taliesin.
>
> **Household project.** Have you been putting off finishing the basement? What better time?
>
> **Medical.** Postponing elective surgery? This may offer the opportunity (make sure that your existing or new health insurance will cover it).
>
> **New residence.** If you need to look for a new house, you may be too busy at the new job to do so for a while after starting. Here is your window.

In any case, unless you cannot afford a gap in your earnings, or your new employer persuades you to start pronto, consider taking a break between jobs, if only a long weekend. Not only is it a chance to rest, but it will help you leave behind one life experience while preparing for another. If you want more than a month before starting the new job, say, make it part of your negotiations. New employers will generally work with you on a mutually acceptable date, even if it means minor inconvenience on their part. Starting a new civil service job can bring lengthy waiting periods, regardless of your timetable. The wheels of government turn s-l-o-w-l-y.

ARCHIVING

What are you supposed to do with that pile of job-hunting-related material that was part of your search? These once-crucial lists, notes, letters, resumes, and photos may seem disposable, but take care before discarding anything. Assemble and sort them, saving the following for future use:

> Work samples: drawings, reports, photos, disks, and other portfolio items.
>
> Resumes: at least one hard copy of each current version, and the electronic files for them.
>
> Correspondence: letters of reference and your letters to employers, references, and colleagues are useful to keep for the future. Even rejection letters from preferred potential employers should be kept (they contain names, addresses, and phone numbers).
>
> Business cards collected while job-hunting, and from your previous job.
>
> Lists: recipients of your resume, and firms who in-

terviewed you. If you maintained a journal or telephone call log as recommended, keep it.
All paperwork to do with your new employer.

Keep work samples and electronic files permanently, and other material for at least 30 days following your start date. You do not want to be set back to square one should something go wrong (or the new job doesn't work out).

FINANCIAL PREPARATIONS

Leaving one payroll for another means reconsidering taxes, pensions, and insurance, and filling out the related forms. Prepare for the paperwork marathon; ask your new employer if you can have the forms at least 48 hours before starting.

Assuming it was not furnished in advance, paperwork concerning personal data, tax withholding, medical coverage, and insurance are among the most common forms you will be asked to fill out, so be ready. Note which ones may require revision later, such as those regarding exemptions or beneficiaries. U.S. residents who are not citizens should bring their green card or work visa, even if they have furnished it previously.

Paperwork for contract employees is usually less extensive than for permanent employees, since contract staff are not employees of the firm they are assigned to. They will receive work contracts and other forms from their employers, frequently by mail, and are expected to fill out and return them expeditiously.

New employees commonly encounter these items for decision:

Tax withholding. Federal form W-2 asks for your total number of deductions. If you have recently had children, purchased or sold a residence, liquidated investments, or received an inheritance, ask your accountant, or someone on the firm's accounting staff for assistance. These changes can substantially affect your deductions, and take-home pay.

Pension contributions. If the employer's pension plan is non-contributory, then there is no choice involved. If you can or must contribute to the plan, decisions are called for. Many employers have pension plans that gradually phase in company-paid contributions. Some contribute every year but will not pay out until the employee is vested, usually a minimum of three years. Sometimes, employees are eligible to contribute to a 401(k) plan shortly after starting. Acquaint yourself with your firm's pension plan, and take full advantage of it. Employee pension contributions are frequently pre-tax—a great incentive to contribute as much as possible. Many plans offer options of investing pension contributions in different funds with differing degrees of risk vs. performance.

Insurance. The most common types of health plans are managed care (HMO), and fee-for-service. Large employers occasionally offer a choice. Some firms include life insurance (usually term) with their benefits package, and this can entail making decisions as to coverage desired and beneficiaries.

ON THE JOB

Once the prep work is completed, what happens? There is work to do both before *and* after the first day. You didn't go through all this effort just to become complacent now. Stay in the groove.

The First Day

Everything is go. Your regular working hours have been established. Leave a little extra travel time in the beginning; a rule of thumb is to add 20 percent to the time you expect it will take. Arriving early will offend no one, and may offer you a small window in which to settle in and compose yourself. It is important to make a good impression, both to employers and to co-workers. Try to remain relaxed, and be yourself. Arriving for the first day of work is like arriving for an interview. Unless you were instructed in advance to report to a specific person, first introduce yourself to the receptionist, or whoever is there and ask for the person who hired you, or for the personnel director.

Whoever comes out to meet you will probably lead you into the main part of the office, perhaps stopping at his or her office or your workspace, or a temporary workspace. Let your greeter do the talking; there will be time for queries later. Find out whom you will be working with. Getting settled can take five minutes or five weeks—just go with the flow. Observe the new office, people, and practice before making assumptions.

Don't bring professional supplies or office decorations—not yet. Wait to see what you will really need and want on the job.

Newcomers can expect some or all of the following introductory ceremonies: Explanation of office policies such as sign-in/sign-out procedures, working hours, and dress code; introductions to co-workers, managers, and principals; an introduction to, and briefing by, your direct supervisor; workspace placement (not necessarily permanent); and an initial work assignment.

When in doubt, it is all right to ask how to fill out a timesheet, where the restroom or photocopier is, how to operate the fax machine, and the like.

Sizing Up a New Employer

Don't judge a new employer on initial appearances. The office is in a glitzy building in an upscale neighborhood; the employer, however, may not necessarily have money to burn. The office is in an old, cramped space: it may have an old lease, with a coveted low rent, or local rents may be too high to acquire new space. Work stations are messy, and staff are wearing jeans—is there a crash effort to meet a deadline? Designers are a motley lot, and eccentricities are almost as much a part of the workaday experience as the work itself. What *should* you pay attention to?

> **Personal work and workload.** Realistic or not? Easy or difficult? Consistent with assignment(s) discussed at interviews?
>
> **Project teammates.** Competent or not? Dedicated or not? Are projects properly staffed?
>
> **Firm-wide workload, current and future.** A space shortage may indicate that the firm is unusually busy. Beginning phases of large projects and stand-by projects may also indicate a good backlog.
>
> **Staff turnover.** High or low? Low indicates staff contentment. High suggests there are better opportunities or wages elsewhere, or working conditions here that are oppressive or onerous.
>
> **Supervision.** Is your supervisor realistic in his or her expectations? Do you get adequate support?
>
> **Principals.** Are they concerned with design tasks,

or are they marketers or managers with little or no studio contact?

Office ambience. Congenial and non-competitive, or tense and anxious?

Technology. Are the hardware and software up-to-date? Is there support staff?

Evaluating your new employer fully will take more than a day. Finding aspects to dislike about a new job is easy; finding its pluses can take longer. You wouldn't want your employer to judge you hastily. Put aside ingrained work habits and pet peeves, at least temporarily. Remember: new people are paid to learn new things.

Settling In

My new job is exciting, challenging, stressful, exhilarating, provocative, frustrating, dull, unfulfilling, arduous, and . . . what else? Emotions tend to run highest at the beginning, and then taper off as the new kid on the block settles in and becomes comfortable with the work environment.

What can you do to ensure acceptance by the firm, and fulfill its expectations?

Show your true colors from the beginning. Do not try to impress anyone with artificial glibness, unnecessary overtime, or chumminess. Don't attempt an intense work effort you cannot sustain.

Maintain a cheerful, can-do attitude. If early assignments seem like drudgery, do not complain. They may be, in part, a test by your employer, and your willingness to undertake them will be considered in your evaluation.

Observe good work habits. Arrive and leave on time, dress presentably, limit non-work-related conversation (including telephone calls) during working hours, respond to requests promptly, and don't take unnecessary time off.

Stay organized. Keep track of all work efforts, maintain files, and be able to quickly retrieve work you have produced. Such simple practices can really impress.

Take care of yourself. If the new job is stressful, you may require more sleep than usual—get it. Eat healthily.

Personal Money Matters

A new job nearly always has new financial implications. Whether it pays more or less than your previous income, there is more to a new position and its wages than may be apparent at first, and "soft" factors may impact your spending patterns.

If your new job entails significantly longer working or travel hours, you will have less free time. This may translate into a need for more conveniences, such as eating out, which costs more. If you've had to move, or purchase a new house or car, you will, temporarily at least, have to economize.

If you have not accumulated a pension, you may want to contribute more of each paycheck to your new retirement plan than you would otherwise—reducing your take-home pay, at least for a while. If you were unemployed and now want to pay down high-interest debts and loans, do not use your savings. If the new job is temporary and you may be faced with an income-less period later, save something to fall back on.

No matter your new financial status, start out fiscally conservative; leave newfound riches alone initially, while you rationally plot your short- and long-range financial strategy. Good investments of capital now will pay handsome rewards later—perhaps more than your current increase in earnings. If you have children, why not start a college fund? Is your car on its last leg? Set aside something for another. Anticipating a deluxe vacation after accumulating some time off? Start a travel fund.

WRAPPING IT UP

Your job-hunting efforts may be over for now. However, there are still a few tasks to attend to.

> Update your resume. The best time to polish it is when there is no pressure, and it will help you remember your initial assignments.
>
> Establish a file for your current job. Use it to save copies of forms and agreements, company policy and benefit booklets, time sheets, and pay stubs. You may need these later, at tax time and if you apply to borrow money.
>
> Contact people who assisted you in your job-hunting effort, tell them of your new job, and thank them for their help. People remember such gratitude.
>
> Help a colleague. If you left a previous employer in good graces, find out if your position has been filled. If not, maybe you know someone who would be interested.
>
> Brush up on professional skills. If your new job requires skills you don't have, now is the time to acquire them. Unless you previously arranged for specialized on-the-job training, you will be expected to learn readily on your own.

And celebrate!

LARGEST 150 ARCHITECTURAL
DESIGN FIRMS IN THE U.S.

Firms are listed in descending order based on annual total revenues.

1. **Gensler**, San Francisco, CA; www.gensler.com
2. **URS**, San Francisco, CA; www.urscorp.com
3. **HOK**, St. Louis, MO; www.hok.com
4. **HKS Inc.**, Dallas TX ; www.hksinc.com
5. **Perkins + Will**, Atlanta, GA; www.perkinswill.com
6. **Skidmore, Owings & Merrill (SOM)**, New York, NY; www.som.com
7. **HDR**, Omaha, NE; www.hdrinc.com
8. **RTKL Associates, Inc.**, Baltimore, MD; www.rtkl.com
9. **Callison**, Seattle, WA; www.callison.com
10. **Perkins Eastman**, New York, NY; www.peapc.com
11. **SmithGroup Inc.**, Detroit, MI; www.smithgroup.com
12. **Kohn Pedersen Fox Associates, PC**, New York, NY; www.kpf.com
13. **Cannon Design**, Grand Island, NY; www.cannondesign.com
14. **NBBJ**, Seattle, WA (M); www.nbbj.com
15. **Leo A. Daly**, Omaha, NE; www.leoadaly.com
16. **Heery International Inc.**, Atlanta, GA; www.heery.com
17. **Zimmer Gunsul Frasca Partnership**, Portland, OR; www.zgf.com
18. **KTGY Group**, Irvine, CA; www.ktgy.com
19. **Gresham Smith & Partners**, Nashville, TN; www.greshamsmith.com
20. **Wimberly Allison Tong & Goo**, Honolulu, HI; www.watg.com
21. **HMC Architects**, Ontario, CA; www.hmcgroup.com
22. **Arquitectonica**, Miami, FL; www.arquitectonica.com
23. **Smallwood Reynolds Stewart Stewart & Associates**, Atlanta, GA; www.srssa.com
24. **Carter & Burgess, Inc.**, Fort Worth, TX; www.c-b.com
25. **Hillier Architecture**, Princeton, NJ; www.hillier.com
26. **Parsons**, Pasadena, CA; www.parsons.com
27. **MulvannyG2 Architecture**, Bellevue, WA; www.mulvannyg2.com

28. **Burt Hill**, Washington, DC; www.burthill.com
29. **DLR Group**, Omaha, NE; www.dlrgroup.com
30. **PageSoutherlandPage**, Houston, TX; www.psp.com
31. **HNTB Cos.**, Kansas City, MO; www.hntb.com
32. **LPA Inc**, Irvine, CA; www.lpainc.com
33. **SHW Group**, Dallas, TX, www.shwgroup.com
34. **SchenkelShultz**, Fort Wayne, IN; www.schenkelshultz.com
35. **NTDStichler Architecture**, San Diego, CA; www.ntd.com
36. **PGAL**, Houston, TX; www.pgal.com
37. **Corgan Associates**, Dallas, TX; www.corgan.com
38. **Perkowitz & Ruth Architects**, Long Beach, CA; www.prarchitects.com
39. **Ellerbe Becket**, Minneapolis, MN; www.ellerbebecket.com
40. **STV Group Inc.**, New York, NY; www.stvinc.com
41. **TranSystems Corp.**, Kansas City, MO; www.transystems.com
42. **CUH2A**, Princeton, NJ; www.cuh2a.com
43. **ThompsonVentulett Stainback & Associates Inc.**, Atlanta, GA; www.tvsa.com
44. **JCJ Architecture**, Hartford, CT; www.jcj.com
45. **PBK Architects**, Houston, TX; www.pbk.com
46. **Moseley Architects**, Richmond, VA; www.moseleyarchitects.com
47. **Little Diversified Architectural Consulting**, Charlotte, NC; www.littleonline.com
48. **OZ Architecture**, Denver, CO; www.ozarch.com
49. **Hammel, Green and Abrahamson**, Minneapolis, MN; www.hga.com
50. **KlingStubbins**, Philadelphia, PA; www.klingstubbins.com
51. **Ewing Cole**, Philadelphia, PA; www.ewingcole.com
52. **Flad & Associates**, Madison, WI; www.flad.com
53. **LS3P Associates**, Charleston, SC; www.ls3p.com
54. **Morris Architects**, Houston, TX; www.morrisarchitects.com
55. **Ware Malcomb**, Irvine, CA; www.waremalcomb.com
56. **TRO Jung/Brannen**, Boston, MA; www.trojungbrannen.com
57. **Chong Partners Architecture**, San Francisco, CA; www.chongpartners.com
58. **Swanke Hayden Connell Architects**, New York, NY; www.shca.com
59. **Elkus Manfredi Architects**, Boston, MA; www.elkusmanfredi.com
60. **WDG Architecture**, Washington, DC; www.wdgarchitecture.com
61. **Davis Brody Bond Aedas**, New York, NY; www.davisbrody.com
62. **Nadel Architects Inc.**, Los Angeles, CA; www.nadelarc.com
63. **Shepley Bulfinch Richardson & Abbott**, Boston, MA; www.shepleybulfinch.com
64. **VOA Associates**, Chicago, IL; www.voa.com
65. **Dewberry**, Fairfax, VA; www.dewberry.com
66. **R.G. Vanderweil Engineers LLP**, Boston, MA; www.vanderweil.com
67. **KKE Architects Inc.**, Minneapolis, MN; www.kke.com
68. **Gould Evans**, Kansas City, MO; www.gouldevans.com
69. **Cooper Carry**, Atlanta, GA; www.coopercarry.com

70. **JMA**, Las Vegas, NV; www.jmaarch.com
71. **Beyer Blinder Belle**; New York, NY; www.beyerblinderbelle.com
72. **Solomon Cordwell Buenz**, Chicago, IL; www.scb.com
73. **Harley Ellis Devereaux**, Southfield, MI; www.harleyellis.com
74. **HLW**, New York, NY; www.hlw.com
75. **FreemanWhite Inc**, Charlotte, NC; www.freemanwhite.com
76. **Niles Bolton Associates**, Atlanta, GA; www.nilesbolton.com
77. **MBH Architects**, Alameda, CA; www.mbharch.com
78. **CO Architects**, Los Angeles, CA; www.coarchitects.com
79. **Opus Group**, Minnetonka, MN; www.opuscorp.com
80. **Einhorn Yaffee Prescott**, Albany, NY; www.eypaedesign.com
81. **WHR Architects**, Houston, TX; www.whrarchitects.com
82. **Fentress Bradburn Architects Ltd.**, Denver, CO; www.fentressbrad-
    burn.com
83. **Cubellis Inc**, Boston, MA; www.cubellis.com
84. **FXFOWLE Architects, PC**, New York, NY; www.fxfowle.com
85. **Paul Steelman Design Group**, Las Vegas, NV; www.paulsteelman.com
86. **OWP/P**, Chicago, IL; www.owpp.com
87. **Polshek Partnership LLP**, New York, NY; www.polshek.com
88. **Karlsberger**, Columbus, OH; www.karlsberger.com
89. **CDI Business Solutions**, Philadelphia, PA; www.cdicorp.com
90. **Bechtel**, San Francisco, CA; www.bechtel.com
91. **S/L/A/M Collaborative Inc.**, Glastonbury, CT; www.slamcoll.com
92. **MCG Architecture**, Pasadena, CA; www.mcgarchitecture.com
93. **Ingenium International Inc.**, Southfield MI; www.theingeniumgroup.com
94. **Costas Kondylis & Partners LLP**, New York, NY; www.kondylis.com
95. **NAC/Architecture**, Seattle, WA; www.nacarchitecture.com
96. **Eppstein Uhen Architects Inc.**, Milwaukee, WI; www.eppsteinuhen.com
97. **Kaplan McLaughlin Diaz**, San Francisco, CA www.kmdarchitects.com
98. **The Durrant Group Inc.**, Dubuque, IA; www.durrant.com
99. **Tsoi/Kobus & Associates Inc.**, Cambridge, MA; www.tka-architects.com
100. **SB Architects**, San Francisco, CA; www.sb-architects.com
101. **Pei Cobb Freed & Partners Architects LLP**, New York, NY; www.pcf-p.com
102. **Dekker/Perich/Sabatini Ltd.**, Albuquerque, NM; www.dpsabq.com
103. **Hnedak Bobo Group**, Memphis, TN; www.hbginc.com
104. **A. Epstein & Sons International**, Chicago, IL; www.epstein-isi.com
105. **Cuningham Group Architecture PA**, Minneapolis, MN; www.cuning-
     ham.com
106. **BSA Lifestructures**, Indianapolis, IN; www.bsalifestructures.com
107. **Michael Baker Corp.**, Moon Twp, PA; www.mbakercorp.com
108. **Steffian Bradley Architects**, Boston, MA; www.steffian.com
109. **ASCG Inc.**, Anchorage, AK; www.ascg.com
110. **BHDP Architecture**, Cincinnati, OH; www.bhdp.com
111. **Crabtree Rohrbaugh & Assoc., Architects**, Mechanicsburg, PA;
     www.cra-architects.com
112. **Fanning/Howey Associates**, Celina, OH; www.fhai.com

113. **Looney Ricks Kiss Architects**, Memphis, TN; www.lrk.com
114. **Astorino**, Pittsburgh, PA; www.astorino.com
115. **GreenbergFarrow**, Atlanta, GA; www.greenbergfarrow.com
116. **SSOE**, Toledo, OH; www.ssoe.com
117. **Arrowstreet**, Somerville, MA; www.arrowstreet.com
118. **H+L Architecture**, Denver, CO; www.hlarch.com
119. **RBB Architects Inc.**, Los Angeles, CA; www.rbbinc.com
120. **EDI Architecture Inc.**, Houston, TX; www.ediarchitecture.com
121. **RNL**, Denver, CO; www.rnldesign.com
122. **CTA Architects Engineers**, Billings, MT; www.ctagroup.com
123. **Carrier Johnson**, San Diego, CA; www.carrierjohnson.com
124. **Payette**, Boston, MA; www.payette.com
125. **FKP Architects Inc**, Houston, TX; www.fkp.com
126. **Stevens & Wilkinson**, Atlanta, GA; www.sw-ga.com
127. **S&B Holdings Ltd. and Affiliates**, Houston, TX; www.sbec.com
128. **HuntonBrady Architects**, Orlando, FL; www.huntonbrady.com
129. **Teng Affiliated Cos.**, Chicago, IL; www.teng.com
130. **The Lawrence Group**, St. Louis, MO; www.thelawrencegroup.com
131. **Westlake Reed Lescosky**, Cleveland, OH; www.vwrl.com
132. **Odell Associates Inc.**, Charlotte, NC; www.odell.com
133. **Bermello Ajamil & Partners**, Miami, FL; www.bermelloajamil.com
134. **Langdon Wilson**, Los Angeles, CA; www.langdonwilson.com
135. **BRPH Architects-Engineers Inc.**, Melbourne, FL; www.brph.com
136. **L. Robert Kimball & Associates**, Ebensburg, PA; www.lrkimball.com
137. **Gruzen Samton LLP**, New York, NY; www.gruzensamton.com
138. **DES Architects & Engineers**, Redwood City, CA; www.des-ae.com
139. **Spector Group**, North Hills, NY (M); www.spectorgroup.com
140. **Ghafari Associates**, Dearborn, MI; www.ghafari.com
141. **Parkhill Smith & Cooper Inc.**, Lubbock, TX; www.team-psc.com
142. **Goodwyn, Mills & Cawood Inc.**, Montgomery, AL; www.gmcnetwork.com
143. **TSP**, Sioux Falls, SD; www.teamtsp.com
144. **Johnson Fain**, Los Angeles, CA; www.johnsonfain.com
145. **Wallace Roberts & Todd LLC**, Philadelphia, PA; www.wrtdesign.com
146. **Lee Burkhart Liu Inc.**, Marina del Ray, CA; www.lblarch.com
147. **Legat Architects Inc.**, Waukegan, IL; www.legat.com
148. **Sasaki Associates**, Watertown, MA; www.sasaki.com
149. **Shalom Baranes Associates, PC**, Washington, DC; www.sbaranes.com
150. **The Neenan Co.**, Fort Collins, CO; www.neenan.com

LARGEST 100 INTERIOR DESIGN
FIRMS IN THE U.S.

Firms are listed in descending order based on total design fees for the previous year.

1. **Gensler**, San Francisco, CA; www.gensler.com
2. **HOK Group**, St. Louis, MO; www.hok.com
3. **Perkins & Will**, Chicago, IL; www.perkinswill.com
4. **Callison**, Seattle, WA; www.callison.com
5. **Nelson & Associates**, Philadelphia, PA; www.nelsononline.com
6. **HDR Architecture**, Omaha, NE; www.hdrinc.com
7. **IA, Interior Architects Inc**, San Francisco, CA; www.interiorarchitects.com
8. **Leo A Daly**, Omaha, NE; www.leodaly.com
9. **Design Forum**, Dayton, OH; www.designforum.com
10. **HBA/Hirsch Bedner Associates**, Los Angeles, CA; www.hbadesign.com
11. **Skidmore Owings & Merrill (SOM)**, New York, NY; www.som.com
12. **Jacobs,** Pasadena, CA; www.jacobs.com
13. **PageSoutherlandPage**, Houston, TX; www.pspaec.com
14. **Cannon Design**, Boston, MA; www.cannondesign.com
15. **Wilson & Associates**, Dallas TX; www.wilsonassoc.com
16. **SmithGroup**, Minneapolis, MN; www.smithgroup.com
17. **Perkins Eastman**, New York, NY; www.peapc.com
18. **TPG (The Phillips Group)**, New York, NY; www.tpgarchitecture.com
19. **NBBJ**, Seattle, WA; www.nbbj.com
20. **Pavlik Design Team**, Ft. Lauderdale, FL; www.pavlikdesign.com
21. **Burt Hill**, Washington, DC; www.burthill.com
22. **DMJM Rottet**, Los Angeles, CA; www.dmjmrottet.com
23. **Rockwell Group**, New York, NY; www.rockwellgroup.com
24. **HLW International**, New York, NY; www.hlw.com
25. **Flad & Associates**, Madison, WI; www.flad.com
26. **FRCH Design Worldwide**, Cincinnati, OH; www.frch.com
27. **KlingStubbins**, Philadelphia, PA; www.klingstubbins.com

28. **Creative Design Consultants**, Costa Mesa, CA; www.cdcdesigns.com
29. **Anshen + Allen**, San Francisco, CA; www.anshen.com
30. **Hillier Architecture**, Princeton, NJ; www.hillier.com
31. **Mancini-Duffy**, New York, NY; www.manciniduffy.com
32. **Zimmer Gunsul Frasca Partnership**, Portland, OR; www.zgf.com
33. **RTKL Associates**, Baltimore, MD; www.rtkl.com
34. **Daroff Design**, Philadelphia, PA; www.daroffdesign.com
35. **Cubellis Associates**, Boston, MA; www.cubellis.com
36. **HKS Inc**, Dallas, TX; www.hksinc.com
37. **Ted Moudis Associates**, New York, NY; www.tedmoudis.com
38. **CUH2A**, Princeton, NJ; www.cuh2a.com
39. **Marc-Michaels Interior Design**, Winter Park, FL; www.marc-michaels.com
40. **Peter Marino Architect**, New York, NY; www.petermarinoarchitect.com
41. **VOA Associates**, Chicago, IL; www.voa.com
42. **A/R Environetics Group**, New York, NY; www.aregroupinc.com
43. **Little**, Charlotte, NC; www.littleonline.com
44. **ASD**, Atlanta, GA; www.asdnet.com
45. **STUDIOS Architecture**, Washington, DC; www.studiosarchitecture.com
46. **HFS/Concepts 4**, Long Beach, CA; www.thehfsgroup.com
47. **Smallwood Reynolds Stewart Stewart**, Atlanta, GA; www.srssa.com
48. **Karlsberger Companies**, Columbus, OH; www.karlsberger.com
49. **Swanke Hayden Connell Architects**, New York, NY; www.shca.com
50. **Brennan Beer Gorman Monk**, New York, NY; www.bbg-bbgm.com
51. **TRO Jung/Brannen**, Boston, MA; www.trojungbrannen.com
52. **DBI Architects**, Washington, DC; www.dbia.com
53. **DiLeonardo International**, Warwick, RI; www.dileonardo.com
54. **OWP/P**, Chicago, IL; www.owpp.com
55. **TVS Interiors**, Atlanta, GA; www.tvsinteriors.com
56. **RMW Architecture & Interiors**, San Francisco, CA; www.rmw.com
57. **CBT/Childs Bertman Tseckares**, Boston, MA; www.cbtarchitects.com
58. **Tricarico Architecture & Design**, Wayne, NJ; www.tricarico.com
59. **Gresham Smith & Partners**, Nashville, TN; www.gspnet.com
60. **The Switzer Group**, New York, NY; www.theswitzergroup.com
61. **Ware Malcomb**, Irvine, CA; www.waremalcomb.com
62. **Planning Design Research Corp.**, Houston, TX; www.pdrcorp.com
63. **Slifer Designs**, Edwards, CO; www.sliferdesigns.com
64. **Group Goetz Architects**, Washington, DC; www.gga.com
65. **PGAL**, Houston, TX; www.pgal.com
66. **Gwathmey Siegel & Associates Architects**, New York, NY; www.gwathmey-siegel.com
67. **Hammel Green & Abrahamson**, Minneapolis, MN; www.hga.com
68. **LS3P Associates**, Charleston, SC; www.ls3p.com
69. **Francis Cauffman Foley Hoffmann**; Philadelphia, PA; www.francis-cauffman.com
70. **Lawrence Group**, St. Louis, MO; www.thelawrencegroup.com

71. **Huntsman Architectural Group**, San Francisco, CA; www.huntsmanag.com
72. **Staffelbach Design Associates**, Dallas, TX; www.staffelbach.com
73. **BraytonHughes Design Studios**, San Francisco, CA; www.bhdstudios.com
74. **McCall Design Group**, San Francisco, CA; www.mccalldesign.com
75. **SPACE**, Chicago, IL; www.thinkspace.biz
76. **The Environments Group**, Chicago, IL; www.envgroup.com
77. **LPA**, Irvine, CA; www.lpainc.com
78. **Rees Associates**, Oklahoma City, OK; www.rees.com
79. **Granary Associates**, Philadelphia, PA; www.granaryassoc.com
80. **Loebl Schlossman & Hackl**, Chicago, IL; www.lshdesign.com
81. **Wimberly Allison Tong & Goo**, Honolulu, HI; www.watg.com
82. **Bergmeyer Associates**, Boston, MA; www.bergmeyer.com
83. **Duncan & Miller Design**, Dallas, TX; www.duncanmillerdesign.com
84. **Sasaki Associates**, Watertown, MA; www.sasaki.com
85. **Gettys**, Chicago, IL; www.gettys.com
86. **WWCOT**, Santa Monica, CA; www.wwcot.com
87. **Baskervill**, Richmond, VA; www.baskervill.com
88. **H. Chambers Co.**, Baltimore, MD; www.chambersusa.com
89. **Babey Moutlton Jue & Booth**, San Francisco, CA; www.bamo.com
90. **Wolcott Architecture Interiors**, Culver City, CA; www.wolcottai.com
91. **Carrier Johnson**, San Diego, CA; www.carrierjohnson.com
92. **Interprise Design**, Addison, TX; www.interprisedesign.com
93. **Ellerbe Becket**, Minneapolis, MN; www.ellerbebecket.com
94. **RYA Design Consultancy**, Dallas, TX; www.rya.com
95. **JRS Architect**, Mineola, NY; www.jrsarchitect.com
96. **Tsoi/Kobus & Associates**, Cambridge, MA; www.tka-architects.com
97. **Elkus/Manfredi Architects**, Boston, MA; www.elkus-manfredi.com
98. **Bilkey Llinas Design**, Palm Beach, FL; www.bilkeyllinas.com
99. **VeenendaalCave**, Atlanta, GA; www.vcave.com
100. **Ronald Schmidt & Associates**, Englewood, NJ; www.rsaaia.com
100. **JGA**, Southfield, MI; www.jga.com

Reproduced from *Interior Design* magazine, January 2007 © 2007 by Reed Business Information.

Duplicate rank number indicates that the firm was tied with the previous.

LARGEST 100
GLOBAL DESIGN FIRMS

Firms are listed in descending order based on the number of design staff. Most are multidisciplinary, and offer architectural and interior design services. These are among the leaders in international design work, and many maintain offices abroad.

1. **Nikken Sekkei**, Tokyo, Japan; www.nikkensekkei.com
2. **Gensler**, San Francisco, CA; www.gensler.com
3. **HOK Group**, St. Louis, MO; www.hok.com
4. **Aedas, London,** UK; www.aedas.com
5. **Skidmore Owings & Merrill (SOM)**, New York, NY; www.som.com
6. **BDP International,** London, UK; www.bdp.co.uk
7. **Perkins & Will**, Chicago, IL; www.perkinswill.com
8. **Foster & Partners**, London, UK; www.fosterandpartners.com
9. **RTKL Associates**, Baltimore, MD; www.rtkl.com
10. **HKS Inc**, Dallas, TX; www.hksinc.com
11. **P & T Group**, Hong Kong; www.p-t-group.com
12. **NBBJ**, Seattle, WA; www.nbbj.com
12. **Perkins Eastman**, New York, NY; www.peapc.com
14. **SmithGroup**, Minneapolis, MN; www.smithgroup.com
15. **Leo A Daly**, Omaha, NE; www.leodaly.com
16. **SMC Group**, London, UK; www.smcgroupplc.com
17. **Kohn Pederson Fox**, New York, NY; www.kpf.com
18. **Callison**, Seattle, WA; www.callison.com
19. **Burt Hill**, Washington, DC; www.burthill.com
20. **Nihon Sekkei**, Tokyo, Japan; www.nihonsekkei.co.jp
21. **Cannon Design**, Grand Island, NY; www.cannondesign.com
22. **RMJM**, London, UK; www.rmjm.co.uk
23. **Kume Sekkei**, Tokyo, Japan; www.kumesekkei.co.jp
24. **The Cox Group**, Sydney NSW, Australia; www.cox.com.au
25. **Hassell**, Sydney NSW, Australia; www.hassell.com.au

26. **Atkins**, Surrey, UK; www.atkinsglobal.com
26. **Woods Bagot**, Adelaide SA, Australia; www.woodsbagot.com.au
28. **Woodhead International**, Adelaide SA, Australia; www.woodhead.com.au
29. **Zimmer Gunsul Frasca Partnership**, Portland, OR; www.zgf.com
30. **DLR Group**, Chicago, IL; www.dlrgroup.com
31. **KlingStubbins**, Philadelphia, PA; www.klingstubbins.com
32. **Capita**, London, UK; www.capitasymonds.co.uk
33. **Chapman Taylor**, London, UK; www.chapmantaylor.com
34. **HBO & EMTB**, Sydney NSW, Australia; www.hboemtb.com
35. **Wimberly Allison Tong & Goo**, Honolulu, HI; www.watg.com
36. **Harley Ellis Devereaux**, Los Angeles, CA; www.harleyellis.com
37. **Leigh & Orange Group**, Hong Kong, China; www.leighorange.com.hk
38. **STUP Consultants**, Mumbai, India; www.stupco.com
39. **Nightingale Associates**, Oxford, UK; www.nightingaleassociates.com
40. **White Arkitekter**, Stockholm, Sweden; www.white.se
41. **Ankrom Moisan Associated Architects**, Portland, OR; www.amaa.com
42. **JSK Architects**, Frankfurt, Germany; www.jsk.de
43. **Smallwood Reynolds Stewart Stewart & Associates**, Atlanta, GA; www.srssa.com
44. **Wong Tung & Partners**; Hong Kong, China; www.wongtung.com
45. **Hillier Architecture**, Princeton, NJ; www.hillier.com
46. **Allies & Morrison**, London, UK; www.alliesandmorrison.co.uk
46. **Ishimoto Architecture & Engineering**, Tokyo, Japan, www.ishimoto.co.jp
48. **Benoy**, London, UK; www.benoy.co.uk
48. **Henn Architekten**, Berlin, Germany; www.henn.com
48. **Reid Architecture**, Birmingham, UK; www.reidarchitecture.com
51. **Thompson Ventulett Stainback & Associates (TVS)**, Atlanta, GA; www.tvsa.com
52. **RKW Rhode Kellerman Wawrowsky**, Dusseldorf, Germany; www.rkw-as.de
52. **Zaha Hadid Architects**, London, UK; www.zaha-hadid.com
54. **Aukett Fitzroy Robinson**, London, UK; www.aukett.com
55. **Arkitektfirmaet CF Møller**, Aarhus, Denmark; www.ark-cfmt.dk
55. **CP Kukreja Associates**, Delhi, India; www.cpkukreja.com
55. **Kaplan McLaughlin Diaz**, San Francisco, CA; www.kmdarchitects.com
55. **Reddy Architecture**, Dublin, Ireland; www.anthonyreddy.com
59. **Broadway Malyan**, London, UK; www.broadwaymalyan.co.uk
60. **Arkitema K/S**, Aarhus, Denmark; www.arkitema.com
60. **KSP Engel & Zimmermann**, Brunswick, Germany; www.ksp-architekten.de
62. **Hamilton Associates Architects Ltd.**, London, UK; www.hamilton-assoc.com
63. **Archetype Group**, Hanoi, Vietnam; www.archetype-group.com
64. **GVA & Associates**, Mexico City, Mexico; www.gva.com.mx
65. **Gould Evans**, Kansas City, MO; www.gouldevans.com
66. **BBG-BBGM**, New York, NY; www.bbg-bbgm.com
67. **Ellerbe Becket**, Minneapolis, MN; www.ellerbebecket.com

68. **WDG Architecture**, Washington, DC; www.wdgarch.com

69. **PRP Architects**, London, UK; www.prparchitects.co.uk

70. **HKR Architects**, Dublin, Ireland; www.hkrarchitects.com

71. **Murray O'Laoire Architects**, Dublin, Ireland; www.murrayolaoire.com

72. **Niles Bolton Associates**, Atlanta, GA; www.nilesbolton.com

73. **Swanke Hayden Connell Architects**, New York, NY; www.shca.com

74. **KKE Architects Inc.**, Minneapolis, MN; www.kke.com

75. **Bates Smart**, Melbourne, Australia; www.batessmart.com.au

76. **Jaspers-Eyers & Partners**, Brussels, Belgium; www.jaspers-eyers.be

76. **Karlsberger,** Columbus, OH; www.karlsberger.com

76. **Lewis & Hickey**, Nottingham, UK; www.lewishickey.com

76. **Stantec Architecture**, Toronto, Ontario, Canada; www.stantec.com

76. **Robbie/Young & Wright Architects**, Toronto, Ontario, Canada; www.rywarch.ca

81. **Sheppard Robson,** London, UK; www.sheppardrobson.com

82. **Coop Himmelblau**, Vienna, Austria; www.coop-himmelblau.at

82. **Langdon Wilson**, Los Angeles, CA; www.langdonwilson.com

82. **Office for Metropolitan Architecture (Rem Koolhaas/OMA)**, Rotterdam, The Netherlands; www.oma.eu

85. **Anshen & Allen**, London, UK; www.anshen.com

85. **Arte Charpentier**, Paris, France; www.arte-charpentier.fr

87. **KEO International Consultants**, Abu Dhabi, UAE; www.keoic.com

88. **Gregotti Associati International**, Milan, Italy; www.gregottiassociati.it

88. **Massimiliano Fuksas Architects**, Rome, Italy; www.fuksas.it

90. **Studios Architecture**, San Francisco, CA; www.studiosarch.com

91. **PRC Group**, London, UK; www.prc-group.com

91. **Schmidt Hammer & Lassen**, Aarhus, Denmark; www.shl.dk

91. **Wilson Associates**, Dallas TX; www.wilsonassoc.com

94. **Design & Architecture Bureau (DAR)**, Dubai, UAE; www.dar.ae

95. **David Chipperfield Architects**, London, UK; www.davidchipperfield.co.uk

95. **Flad & Associates**, Madison, WI; www.flad.com

95. **Hopkins Architects**, London, UK; www.hopkins.co.uk

98. **Austin-Smith:Lord**, London, UK; www.austinsmithlord.com

99. **Zeidler Partnership Architects**, Toronto, Ontario, Canada; www.zrpa.com

100. **Diamond & Schmitt Architects**, Toronto, Ontario, Canada; www.dsai.ca

First published by Building Design's *BD World Architecture 100 Magazine,* January 2007.

Duplicate rank numbers indicate that the firm was tied with the previous.

LARGEST 100 DESIGN-BUILD
FIRMS IN THE U.S.

Firms are listed in descending order based on annual revenue from design-build contracts.

1. **Bechtel**, San Francisco, CA; www.bechtel.com
2. **Fluor Corp.**, Aliso Viejo, CA; www.fluor.com
3. **Jacobs**, Pasadena, CA; www.jacobs.com
4. **CB&I** (Chicago Bridge & Iron Co.), The Woodlands, TX; www.cbi.com
5. **McDermott International Inc.**, Houston, TX; www.mcdermott.com
6. **Black & Veatch**, Kansas City, MO; www.bv.com
7. **CH2M Hill Cos.**, Englewood, CO; www.ch2m.com
8. **Opus Group**, Minnetonka, MN; www.opuscorp.com
9. **Foster Wheeler Ltd.**, Clinton, NJ; www.fosterwheeler.com
10. **Kiewit Corp.**, Omaha, NE; www.kiewit.com
11. **Parsons**, Pasadena, CA; www.parsons.com
12. **Washington Group International Inc.**, Boise, ID; www.wgint.com
13. **Fagen Inc**, Granite Falls, MN; www.fageninc.com
14. **Clark Group**, Bethesda, MD; www.clarkconstruction.com
15. **KBR**, Houston, TX; www.kbr.com
16. **Duke Construction**, Indianapolis, IN; www.dukeconstructiononline.com
17. **The Shaw Group Inc.**, Baton Rouge, LA; www.shawgrp.com
18. **Hensel Phelps Construction Co.**, Greeley, CO; www.henselphelps.com
19. **Panattoni Construction Inc.**, Sacramento, CA; www.panattoni.com
20. **Zachry Construction Corp**, San Antonio, TX; www.zachry.com
21. **Clayco**, St. Louis, MO; www.claycorp.com
22. **Ryan Cos.**, Minneapolis, MN; www.ryancompanies.com
23. **Lauth Group Inc**, Indianapolis, IN; www.lauthproperty.com
24. **Stellar**, Jacksonville, FL; www.tsgjax.com
25. **The Haskell Co.**, Jacksonville, FL; www.thehaskellco.com
26. **S&B Holdings LTD**, Houston, TX; www.sbec.com
27. **Earth Tech Inc**, Long Beach, CA; www.earthtech.com

28. **Burns & McDonnell**, Kansas City, MO; www.burnsmcdonnell.com
29. **MWH Global**, Broomfield, CO; www.mwhglobal.com
30. **HBE Corp.**, St. Louis, MO; www.hbecorp.com
31. **The Turner Corp.**, Dallas, TX; www.turnerconstruction.com
32. **Webcor Builders**, San Mateo, CA; www.webcor.com
33. **M.A. Mortenson Co.**, Minneapolis, MN; www.mortenson.com
34. **PCL Construction Enterprises Inc.**, Denver, CO; www.pcl.com
35. **MACTEC Inc**, Alpharetta, GA; www.mactec.com
36. **Hunt Building Corp.**, El Paso, TX; www.huntbuilding.com
37. **McGough Cos.**, St. Paul, MN; www.mcgough.com
38. **Skanska USA Inc**, Whitestone, NY; www.skanska.com
39. **The Facility Group**, Smyrna, GA; www.facilitygroup.com
40. **The Hanover Co**, Houston, TX; www.hanoverco.com
41. **BE & K Inc.**, Birmingham, AL; www.bek.com
42. **The McShane Cos.**, Rosemont, IL; www.mcshane.com
43. **ABB Lummus Global**, Bloomfield, NJ; www.abb.com/lummus
44. **H & M Co. Inc.**, Jackson, TN; www.hmcompany.com
45. **Gray Construction**, Lexington, KY; www.jngray.com
46. **McCarthy Bldg. Cos. Inc.**, St. Louis. MO; www.mccarthy.com
47. **Morley Builders**, Santa Monica, CA; www.morleybuilders.com
48. **Herzog Contracting Corp.**, St. Joseph, MO; www.herzogcompanies.com
49. **R & O Construction**, Ogden, UT; www.randoco.com
50. **The Walsh Group Ltd.**, Chicago, IL; www.walshgroup.com
51. **Swinerton Inc.**, San Francisco, CA; www.swinerton.com
52. **Caddell Construction**, Montgomery, AL; www.caddell.com
53. **Brinderson**, Costa Mesa, CA; www.brinderson.com
54. **DPR Construction Inc.**, Redwood City, CA; www.dprinc.com
55. **Cajun Constructors**, Baton Rouge, LA; www.cajunusa.com
56. **Tellepsen**, Houston, TX; www.tellepsen.com
57. **CDM**, Cambridge, MA; www.cdm.com
58. **Messer Construction Co.**, Cincinnati, OH; www.messer.com
59. **Marshall Erdman & Associates Inc.**, Madison, WI; www.marshallerdman.com
60. **B.L. Harbert International**, Birmingham, AL; www.blharbert.com
61. **FCL Builders Inc**, Itasca, IL; www.fclbuilders.com
62. **The Whiting-Turner Contracting Co.**, Baltimore, MD; www.whiting-turner.com
63. **BBL Construction Services LLC**, Albany, NY; www.bblinc.com
64. **Contrack International Inc**, Arlington, VA; www.contrack.com
65. **Balfour Beatty Construction Inc**, Atlanta, GA; www.balfourbeatty.com
66. **Tutor-Saliba Corp.**, Sylmar, CA; www.tutorsaliba.com
67. **The Korte Co.**, St. Louis, MO; www.korteco.com
68. **Perini Corp.**, Framingham, MA; www.perini.com
69. **Flatiron Construction**, Longmont, CO; www.flatironcorp.com
70. **Sundt Construction Inc.**, Tempe, AZ; www.sundt.com
71. **Fru-Con Construction**, St. Louis, MO; www.fru-con.com

72. **Hunt Construction Group**, Scottsdale, AZ; www.huntconstruction-group.com
73. **Jones Lang LaSalle**, Boston, MA; www.joneslanglasalle.com
74. **CR Meyer**, Oshkosh, WI; www.crmeyer.com
75. **Kinsley Construction Inc.**, York, PA; www.rkinsley.com
76. **M + W Zander U.S. Operations Inc.**, Plano, TX; www.mw-zander.us
77. **Bovis Lend Lease**, New York, NY; www.bovislendlease.com
78. **Matthews Construction Co. Inc.**, Conover, NC; www.matthewsconstruction.com
79. **Oltmans Construction Co.**, Whittier, CA; www.oltmans.com
80. **Choate Construction Co.**, Atlanta, GA; www.choateco.com
81. **Brinkmann Constructors**, Chesterfield, MO; www.rgbrinkmann.com
82. **Albert C. Kobayashi Inc.**, Waipahu, HI; www.ack-inc.com
83. **Armada Hoffler Construction Co**, Virginia Beach, VA; www.armada-hoffler.com
84. **Harper Construction Co. Inc.**, San Diego. CA (no Web site)
85. **XL Construction Corp.**, Milpitas, CA; www.xlconstruction.com
85. **Howard S. Wright Construction Co**, Seattle, WA; www.howardswright.com
87. **Hunzinger Construction Co.**, Brookfield, WI; www.hunzinger.com
88. **Welbro Building Corp.**, Maitland, FL; www.welbro.com
89. **J.E. Dunn Construction Group**, Kansas City, MO; www.jedunn.com
90. **Klinger Cos. Inc.**, Sioux City, IA; www.klinger-companies.com
91. **Corrpro Cos. Inc**, Medina, OH; www.corrpro.com
92. **The Austin Co.**, Cleveland, OH; www.theaustin.com
93. **Devcon Construction Inc.**, Milpitas, CA; www.devconconstruction.com
94. **Industrial Contractors Inc.**, Evansville, IN; www.industrialcontractors.com
95. **VCC**, Little Rock, AR; www.vccusa.com
96. **Alberici Corp.**, St. Louis, MO; www.alberici.com
97. **Gilbane Building Co.**, Providence, RI; www.gilbanebuilding.com
98. **Sahara Inc.**, West Bountiful, UT; www.saharaconstruction.com
99. **Barton Malow Co.**, Southfield, MI; www.bartonmalow.com
100. **The Neenan Co.**, Fort Collins, CO; www.neenan.com

INDEX

National Council of Architectural
Registration Boards, 31
networking, 41–43
new job, 175–185
    evaluation of new employer,
        182–83
    financial considerations, 184
    first day, 181–82
    preparing to start, 175–80
    settling in, 183–84
newsletters, 38–39
newspaper classifieds, 43–44

online research, 26
    commercial web sites, 27–28
    contract employers, 47–48
    dedicated job web sites, 30–31
    employer Web sites, 31–33
    goals, 27
    international firms, 34–35
    internship opportunities, 31
    public job websites, 29
    public solicitations, 29–30
    search engines, 27
    search techniques, 28, 33–35
operations management, 57
overtime policies, 139, 150

past employment, descriptions of,
    56–57
pension plans, 139
per diem travel allowances, 158, 171
permanent positions, 123
personal contacts
    connection with potential em-
        ployer, 89–91
    interview based on referral, 115
    professional inquiries, 39–40
    references, 108–9, 131
phone book search, 44–45
photographs, portfolio, 99
placement services, 45–46
planning services, 62–63
political advocacy, 13

portfolios
    contents, 97, 98–99
    digital content, 101–2
    drawings, 99–101
    interview process, 128
    photographs, 99
    purpose, 97
    saving, 178
    work samples vs., 98
    writing samples, 101
pre-design services, 55
preparation
    consideration of professional hi-
        erarchy, 22–23
    entry-level job search, 19–20
    goal-setting, 16–17
    for interview, 116
    mental attitude, 15
    resume-writing, 88–89
    seeing employer's perspective,
        16, 17–19
    before starting new job, 175–80
    see also research
production-oriented designers, 18
program management, 66
project management, 56, 60
publishers, 82–83

quality assurance officer, 60

real estate development, 75–76
record keeping
    archiving job search-related ma-
        terials, 178–79
    during job search, 25–26
    resume records, 96–97
references, 108–9, 131. see also per-
    sonal contacts
referral for interview, 115
regional planning, 62
relocation for work
    advantages, 155–56
    business trends, 153, 154–55
    cultural adjustment, 168–70, 174